Productive Learning with Microsoft Learning Suite

Build Your Own Learning Experience with Microsoft Learning Suite

Ridi Ferdiana
Lulu Publisher

Lulu Publisher, License Notes.
Productive Learning with Microsoft Learning Suite

ISBN-13 (pbk): 978-1-300-64129-2

Lead Editor : Obert Hoseanto
Technical Reviewer : PIL-Indonesia Division
Cover Designer : Lulu Publisher and Novrian Fajar

First Printing : January 2013
Lulu Enterprises, Inc.

ACKNOWLEDGEMENTS

Above all others, this book is for my family: **Chichi, Mom, Dad,** and my **Sister.** Author would like to thank to MIC team (http://micresearch.net), who give the author a better design cover and nicely links and screenshot.

Author would also like to thank to Gadjah Mada University (http://te.ugm.ac.id), without a good place to work, this work would never have been completed. Finally yet importantly, this book is for teacher community who love to learn and changes the world with education. Enjoy this book and reach me at ridi@mvps.org if you have something to share.

Regards

Ridi

CONTENTS

1 Prologue

1.1 Life Long Learning

Learning is about gathering understanding from the others. There are six pillars of learning which are learning to life, learning to know, learning to do, learning to be, learning to change, and learning to create sustainable development. Nowadays, people has several learning option such as classroom, e-learning, one-on-one coaching, and continuing education. The combination between the two will create lifelong learning with many options available.

Educational organization like school and university already implement a learning method to make learning experience is enjoyable. However, we see a lot that learning in academic is about lecturing activities when teacher talk too much and student hear too much. Lecturing is the most effective method but sometime make our student bored.

In this book, it is discussed tools and techniques to make learning experience more enjoyable. The purposes of this book is to enable a teacher, lecturer, or student to learn and share anything through ICT media. This book is for you if

1. You are teacher and lecturer who shares any good information to the student.
2. You are writer or journalist who shares many publication to the internet or newspaper/
3. You are student who creates a paper, writes a thesis, or create a homework.
4. You are personal who like and enjoy to learn and write any subject.

In this book, it will cover several phases to create a learning productivity. In this book, it will be divided into several steps which are:

1. Research phase. This phase will help you to do a research about something. It will go through searching technique, finding academic research paper, and exploring much through specific tools. Chapter 2 will explain the research phase further.
2. Creating phase. This phase will cover you a global step to create your learning content. Learning content can be considered as a medium to learn and to share. In this chapter, it will cover several productivity software to create notes, present your idea, creating collage, and designing 3D photo. Chapter 3 will cover this creating phase.
3. Collaboration phase. This phase will cover several techniques to manage collaboration in order to gain better understanding in learning. This phase will be described in Chapter 4.

4. Sharing phase. This phase discuss the sharing process and technique. In this phase, it is shown that several techniques and discipline can be done to get better learning outcome. This phase will be described in Chapter 5.

In the end of this book, it will discuss any opportunity that we can use to facilitate and improve our learning experience with the others peers through online community and specific program.

1.2 Learning with a Technology

The first question of this chapter are “Do you have a computer?” Learning with a technology is just like learning with your computer. Computer provides you software to compute and to communicate with the others using internet channel.

Basically, this book need a computer and also a software like operating system or productivity software. In this book, it is assumed that you already own a computer with this hardware requirements.

- A computer with a processor 1 GHz or better
- 2 GB Ram or better
- Sufficient hard disk, 128 GB or more is recommended
- Any display adapter that can works
- Monitor with resolution better than 1024 x 768 pixel
- Input devices like Keyboard, Mouse, and Web-camera

The computer should also configured well with a several software like

- Windows Vista or better operating system like Windows 7 or Windows 8. You can download Windows 8 Trial here http://bit.ly/w8trial
- Office 2007 or better like Office 2010 or Office 2013. You can download Office 2013 trial here http://bit.ly/office2013trial
- Microsoft Learning Suite. Learning suite by Microsoft provides you a bunch of free software that can be used to learn and to teach. You can download the software for free by joining the network and visiting this site http://bit.ly/pillearningsuite
- Windows Essentials. Windows Essentials is a free software from Microsoft that provides you multimedia software like photo gallery, video editor, and blogging software. You can download the Windows Essentials here http://bit.ly/wessentials

If you don’t have the software listed above, just click the link, download the software and you won’t regret your investment to get better learning productivity. If you already download the software, you can install it later along with this book chapter. In the rest of this book, you might know several software that can be downloaded for free, some of software will give you additional benefit for portion of a chapter. You are ready to go for the next chapter if you already have Windows operating system.

Productive Learning with Microsoft Learning Suite

2 Conducting a Research

2.1 Search Anything with Search Engine

Anybody love to search, that's why Bing, Google, and Yahoo provides better search engine day by day. Search engine can help you a lot when you want to search almost anything. Nowadays, search engine can search various kind of content such as webpage, document, music, video, and local business. Figure 1 shows how Bing can search various type of content.

Figure 1 Bing search engine at http://bing.com

In Figure 1, you can search by selecting the category in the right menu and text the keywords in the textbox. The result will be displayed in the others pages. There are important things that you need to consider when you do a search which are:

1. Keywords selection, the keyword is the main things that you should care. Selecting right keyword will give you better result.
2. Content type, content type will limit the search result within the content type. For example, if you search a video in the web content you will get less rather than use videos tabs.
3. Result Filter, result filter sometime limit the search result to give proper result for audience. Removing filter result can help you get better search result, but in return you might get improper result such as violence, gore, and mature content.

Let's do a simple exercise. Let see you want to search any kind information about "Rotary engine". We will use Bing search engine to shows the related information about Rotary engine.

1. Open your favorite search engine, for example in this lab we will use Bing that can be accessed through http://bing.com
2. Let's we search the common type of content, so we will choose Web content.
3. If you need to find a global information about the topic you can use 5W-1H technique. You can start type your search engine with What, Who, Where, Why, When, and How. If you start from

beginning start searching by what keyword that followed with a keywords (i.e. "What is rotary engine"). Search engine never care about your grammar so you can type what you want and luckily it can suggest your keyword. Figure 2 shows the search result when we type "what is rotary engine"

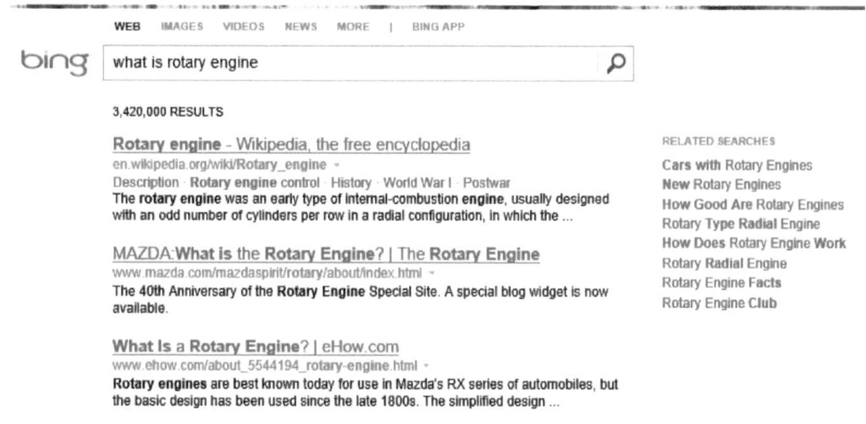

Figure 2 Search result page on Bing

4. After we got the result explore each link by using open in new tab option. To do that just right click in the link and choose "open in a new tab". Please note that any browser has different behavior so you might find equal sentences to open in new tab.

5. Search engine do a search based on popularity, content complexity, and content owner.

6. Using a same keywords, we can search another type of content such as images, video, and news. Images will show the list of images that related with a keyword. Videos will tell you the various video that related with keywords. News will show the current news that related with the keywords.

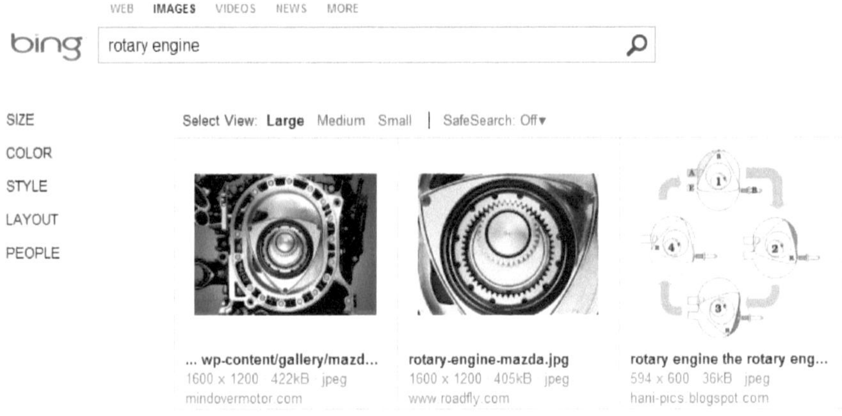

Figure 3 Image type searching

7. You can limit the search result by providing several filter such as size, color, and style. In video, you can search by video source, length, and resolution.

8. If you need more result you can turn of the safe search. But please be careful that some of improper content will show and it won't be good for education or informational purposes.

9. If you wish to find a PDF document, you can search by inserting "rotary engine filetype:pdf". You can change to another type for example word document (doc), spreadsheet (xlsx), or presentation file (pptx). Figure 4 shows the result when we type "rotary engine filetype:pdf".

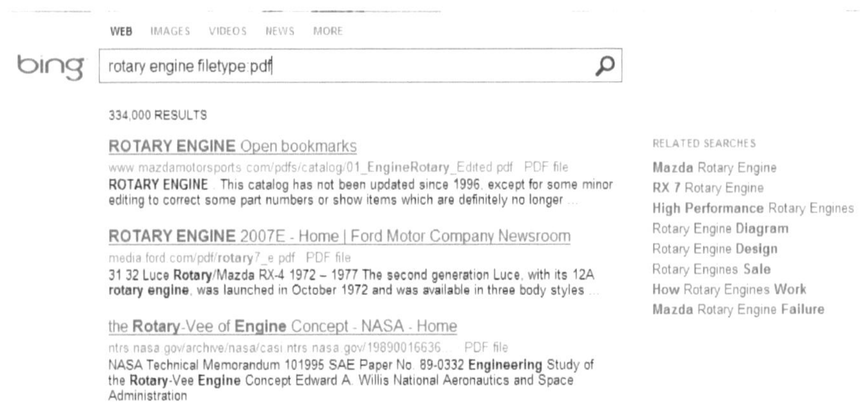

Figure 4 Content searching using file type

10. Make it as a bookmark, if you are a searching fan. It is a good idea to make a search engine as your homepage. For example, in Internet option you can do this by visiting internet options, general tab, and copy paste your homepage as shown in Figure 5.

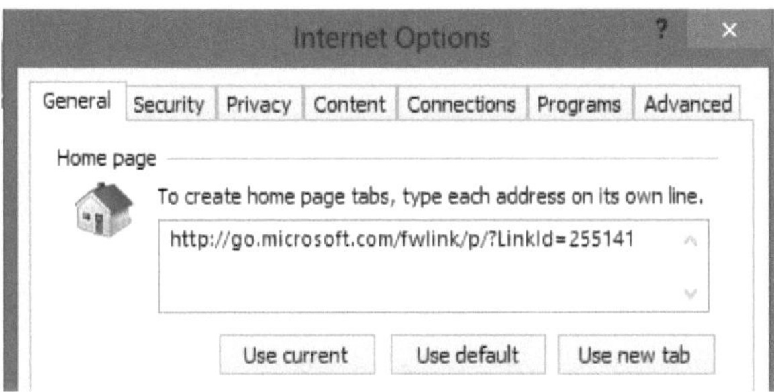

Figure 5 setting a homepage

11. The others option is to install a Bing toolbar. Bing toolbar is a modern way to search and get in touch your search activity with social media. You can grab it free as a plugin for your browser at http://toolbar.discoverbing.com

Search engine is a dedicated website to find anything in the World Wide Web. If you plan to search a specific content such as research paper, academic publication, or conference proceeding, you can use specific search engine. This kind of search engine will be discussed in the Section 2.2.

2.2 Performing Academic Search

As a researcher and a learner, you should learn from the past and improve for the future. If you need a specific research paper you can find it using specific search engine such as Microsoft Academic Search Engine. In this Section, we will provide a step-by-step searching experience by using Microsoft Academic Search.

1. You can start search a research paper or an academic publication by visiting the URL http://academic.research.microsoft.com/ . Figure 6 shown

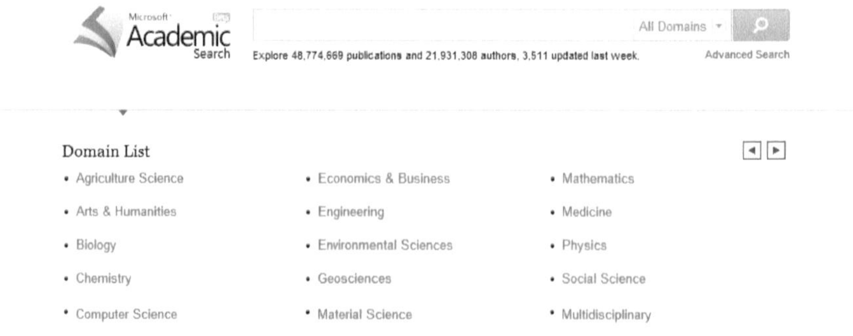

Figure 6 Microsoft Academic Search

2. Microsoft Academic Search (MAS) provides a casual search engine with result limitation on academic result. For example, we will search a "software engineering" keyword. Figure 7 shows the search result. As shown in Figure 7, MAS will show a publication trend, authors list, related conferences, context definition, related keywords, and publication.

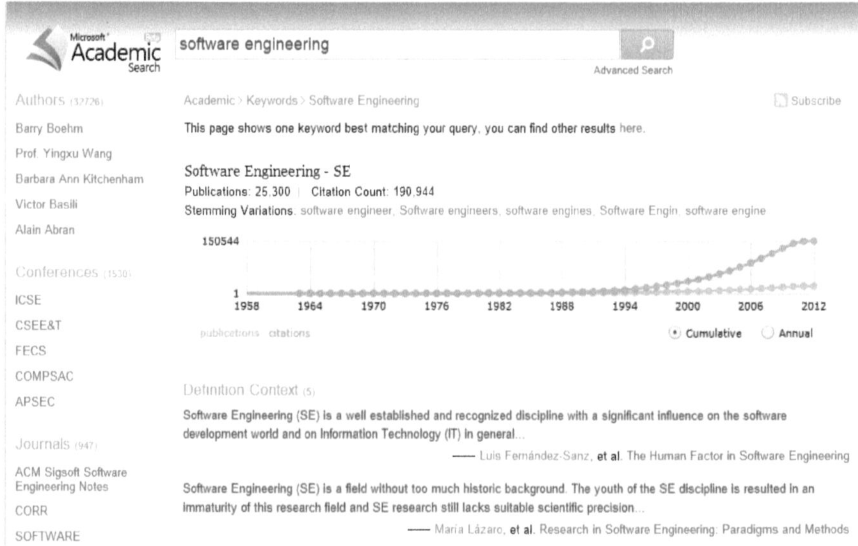

Figure 7 Searching in MAS

3. If we click one of the publication. We will see the abstract, the publisher, the content (if permitted), and related references. The paper can also be exported to references system such as BibTex, RIS, and RefWorks. You can export the references by clicking the export format.

4. Several publication can be downloaded directly, you can see a pdf logo that show you can see their publication. In others hand, if you see no downloadable content, it means you should subscribe to a digital library publication like ACM (http://dl.acm.org), IEEE (http://ieee.org).

5. Publication is a great way to learn about something interested in academic field. You can also find the latest trend of publication by seeing the visualization trend. There are academic map, domain trend, and others. For example, domain trend shows what a great topic in a year. Figure 8 shows the domain trend in computer science.

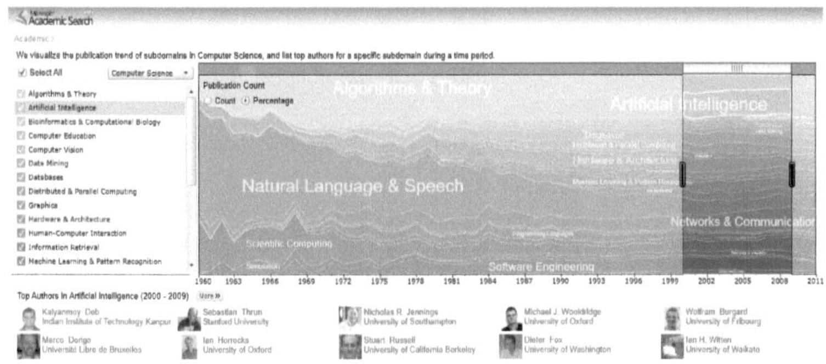

Figure 8 Domain trend in MAS

6. Beside MAS, you can search others publication and research publication in Directory of Open Access Journal (DOAJ). DOAJ is a portal that aggregate any journal that can be published online without subscription fee. You can visit DOAJ at http://www.doaj.org/ . Figure 9 shows the web interface of DOAJ.

7. As a search engine, DOAJ will redirect you to a journal publisher. You can download the paper for free.

Figure 9 Searching in Open Access Journal

Academic search focuses to get academic content for further research. Student or teacher can use academic search to filter the web search result into more valid academic content.

2.3 Software for Research

Several software is built for research purposes. For example, Microsoft learning suite is set of software that provide a teacher and a student to explore a lot research activities. In this section, it will show you what Microsoft learning suite is and how to get it for free.

1. In order to get Microsoft Learning suite, you should join Partners in Learning network (PIL-Network). PIL-Network can be visited at http://pil-network.com. It provides you a learning resources, community, and. Please see Chapter 6 for further information in registering and utilizing PIL-Network

2. Visit the Resources page and click the free tools. Figure 10 shows the Free Tools page.

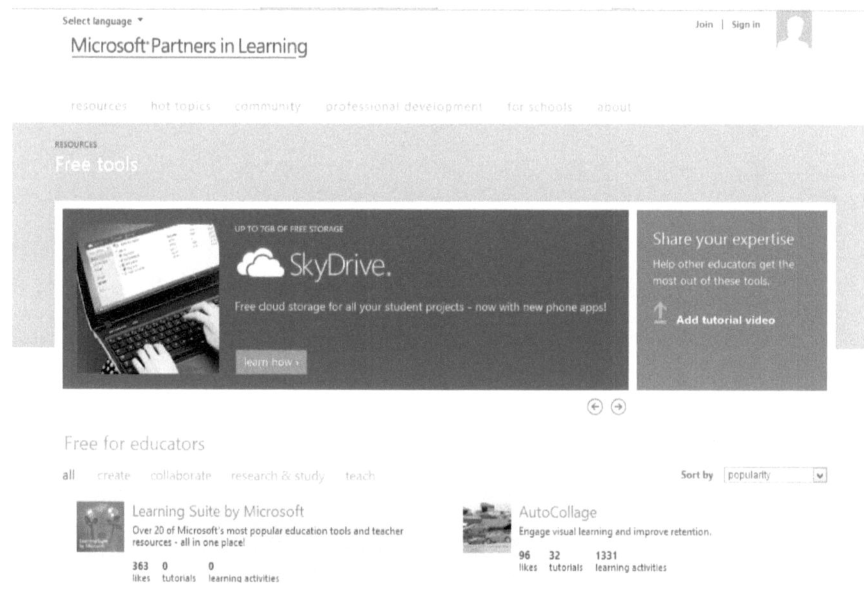

Figure 10 Resources page on PIL-Network

3. Some software is aggregated in a software called learning suite and the rest can be downloaded separately. Software like OneNote, Windows Kinect SDK, and others can be downloaded by clicking the icon of the software.

4. The resources page is divided into four main resource categories which are create category, collaborate category, research and study category, and teaching category. This section will focus in Research and Study category. Therefore, you can click the research and study category.

5. Research and study category shows several software such as Microsoft Mathematics, Worldwide telescope, Sticky sorter, and more. You can download and use without charge but you must register first.

6. As an example for this section, we will download the Worldwide telescope (WWT). WWT is a research software to explore outer space in a PC and internet connection. You can click the worldwide telescope and select "get it now". You will be redirected to Official WWT site. You can start the installation by clicking "Install Worldwide Telescope". Figure 11 shows the WWT website.

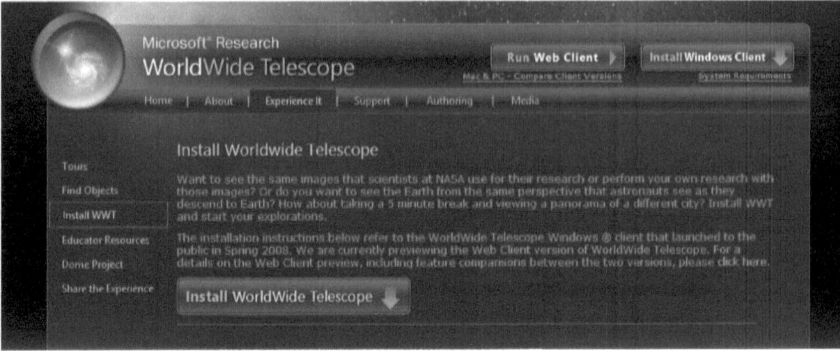

Figure 11 Install Worldwide Telescope

7. The installation is quite simple, you will be offered an excel add-in and automatic update feature. You can install as usual, clicking next for some options and the WWT will installed on your computer. Figure 12 shows the WWT icon includes a Mars icon for WWT.

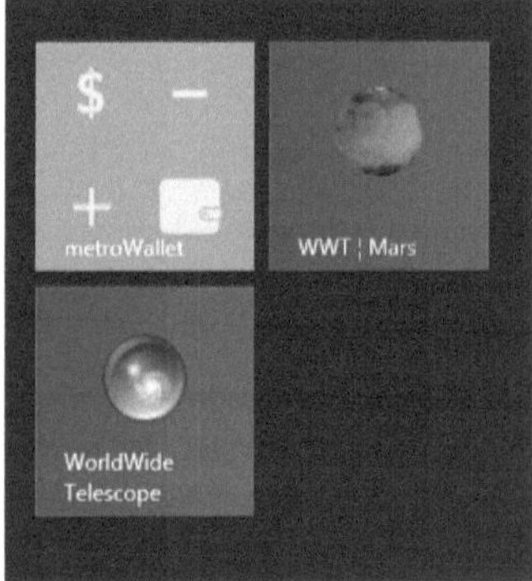

Figure 12 WWT Icons

8. As shown in Figure 12, we will click the Worldwide Telescope icon. If this is your first launch of your WWT, you shall see that WWT need to access the internet and need your permission for the firewall access.

9. There are plenty options available but there are only two mode that you can learn WWT. The first mode is free exploration and the second mode is guided exploration. We will try the second one. Guided tour can be selected by clicking Guided Tours from upper menu. Figure 13 shows several guided tours that are available in WWT.

Figure 13 WWT Guided tours

10. For this lab, let's we click Supernova. The WWT will load the tours that related with Supernova. You can play the tours and hear the multimedia content that available. WWT is updated regularly. The WWT will connect to the internet and grab the new contents when it is available.

11. You can use your keyboard and mouse to navigate the content like a planet, star, and others. Figure 14 shows the navigation model on WWT.

Figure 14 WWT Navigation Model

3 Create Learning Material

3.1 Taking Notes in Any Learning Activities

In learning, creating notes will help student and teacher to understand the courses, to remember the important fact, and to make a short reminder for certain topic. Frankly speaking, creating notes will help student and teacher gain same vision about the courses. In this section we will focus in note creation using OneNote and Sticky Sorter. Both software can be downloaded in http://pil-network.com. This section will focus in two basic operation for OneNote and Sticky Sorter. We start from the simple one which is Stick Sorter.

3.1.1 Sticky Sorter

Sticky sorter is a full featured sticky notes that can be used for free. It just like Windows Sticky Notes but provides more features. Please follow these steps to download and use the Sticky Sorter.

1. You should login to PILN and then navigate to http://www.pil-network.com/resources/tools
2. You should find Sticky Sorter product as shown in Figure 15. You can download it at http://bit.ly/13a5KJ6

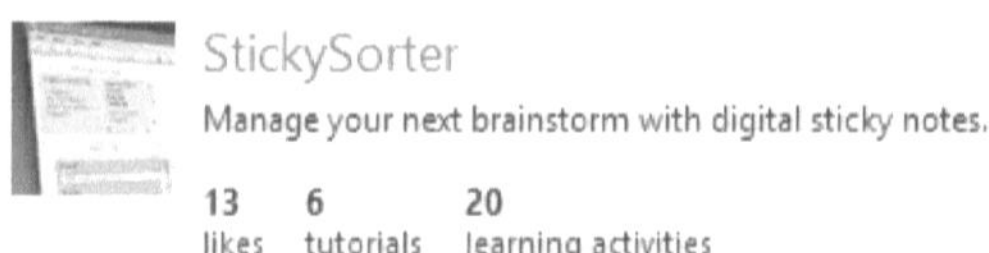

Figure 15 Sticky Sorter Download Page

3. Installation is quite easy and you can run the Sticky Sorter. Sticky Sorter helps student or teacher take a short notes about anything important that should be remembered. This Sticky Sorter have an ability to sort and group the notes as you need. Let's we try the application by adding several notes. You can do that by clicking add notes icon as shown in Figure 16.

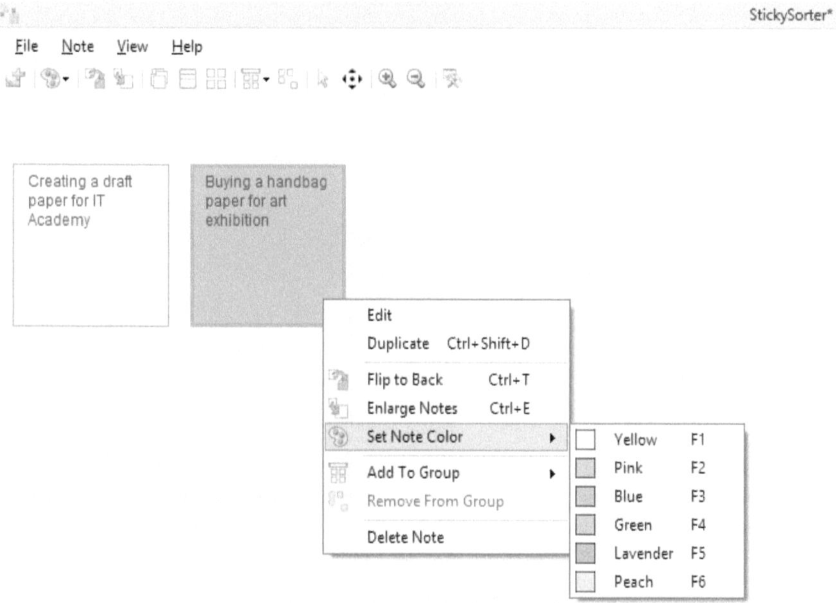

Figure 16 Sticky Sorter Application

4. As shown in Figure 16, you can give different color using F1-F6 keyboard shortcut. You can enlarge the notes, flipping the notes, and group the notes. Let's try to add a group by right clicking in empty screen and create group.

5. After creating a group, you can categorize the notes based on a group. You can do that by right clicking the notes and add to group. The group label will be stored in back page of the notes.

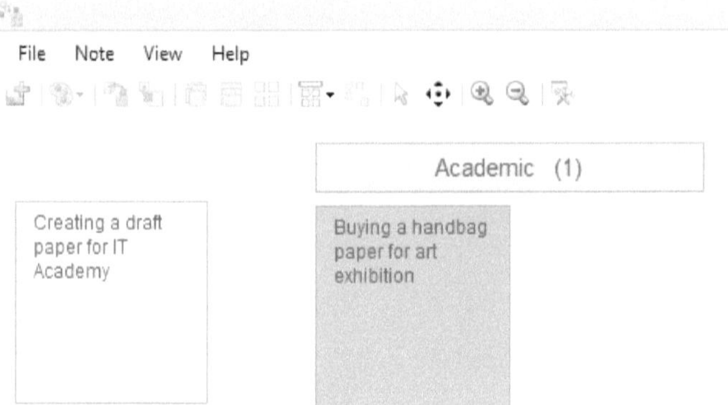

Figure 17 Grouping a sticky notes

6. Sticky Sorter can be used for student to remember the task or to restate their target. You can create a set of sticky notes and save it as CSV (comma separated value). It means that we can manage more than one sticky notes. Sticky sorter might not a good way to take a complex notes but it a good way to manage tasks.

7. A good practice when using a sticky not is when you get “AHA” condition or to put a notes for any tasks that need to be done later.

3.1.2 OneNote

In the past, we love to bring our physical notebook as a tool for note taking. Notebook is a note taking book that contains pages that divided into several sections. Each section will have several pages just like notebook. Figure 17 shows a conventional notebook that you usually bring to your class.

OneNote is an application that behave like your conventional notebook that run on your Windows, Windows Phone, Mac, or even Android. You can use the OneNote to take any notes and read it in any supported devices that can synchronized within internet. OneNote provides a fruitful features rather than conventional notebook such as an ability to record multimedia notes, an ability to share the notebook to the peers, and an ability to collaborate with the others. You can download the trial of OneNote at http://bit.ly/onenotetrial or you can bought at Amazon http://bit.ly/buyonenote

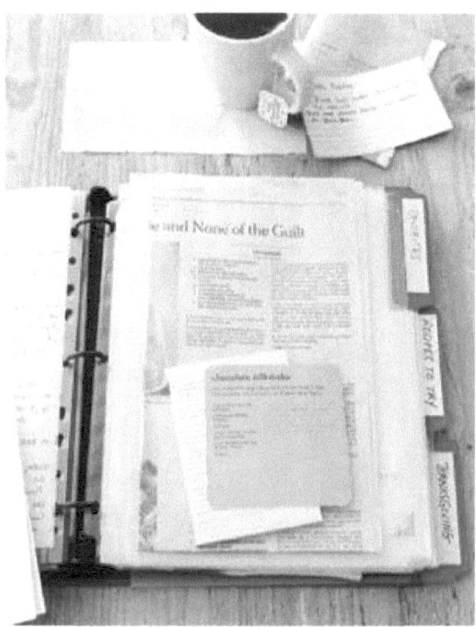

Figure 18 Conventional Notebook

In this section we will learn a basic OneNote operation which are creating a notebook, editing the notes, and sharing to the others. Let's start by installing OneNote and start the tutorial below.

1. In this article, it will use OneNote 2013. The latest OneNote that we have in the market. You can start the OneNote by clicking the OneNote 2013 icon as shown in Figure 19. Figure 19 shows basic feature of OneNote which are the OneNote itself and Send to OneNote. Send to OneNote works best in term of integration with the others application. For example, you can save an html page in OneNote, screen clipping your computer, even creating a quick note.

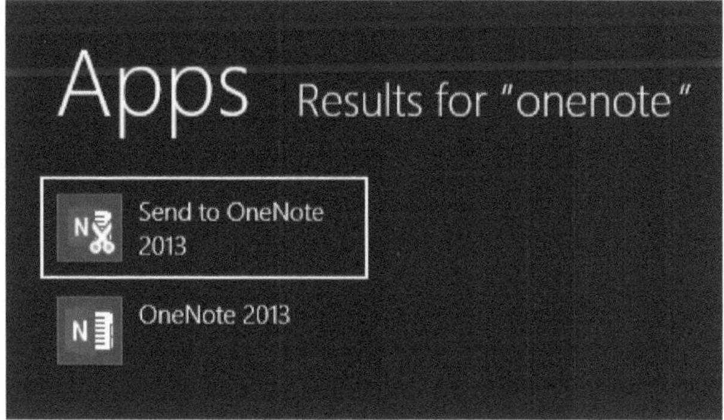

Figure 19 OneNote 2013 icon

2. If we click Send to OneNote, we will find three main menu which are Screen Clipping (Windows Key + S), Send to OneNote (Windows Key + D), and Create a quick notes (Windows Key + N). Let's we try Windows Key + S. You will get a white screen and you can select a screenshot region. It's working like print screen but with and advanced features like storing the result to clipboard or to OneNote. Figure 20 shows send to OneNote utility, this handy tool will help to capture any information from your computer.

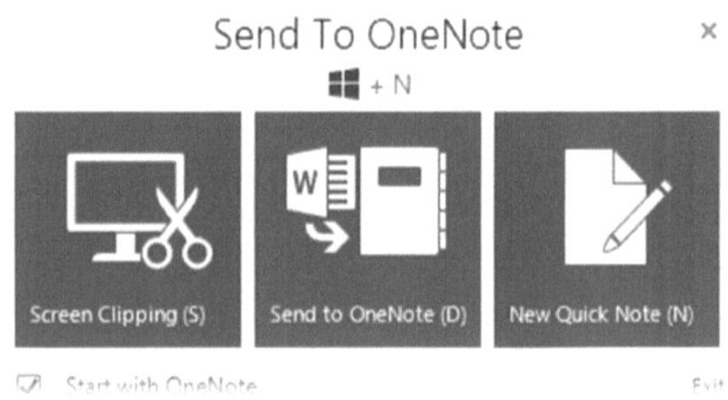

Figure 20 OneNote Send to OneNote

3. OneNote is powerful app to manage our notes. In order to create a new notebook, open file → new notebook. As shown in Figure 21, we can choose the storage for our notebook which are on local computer, SkyDrive, or Office 365 SharePoint. In this tutorial, we create a local notebook. Let's submit a notebook name called : MyResearchLog

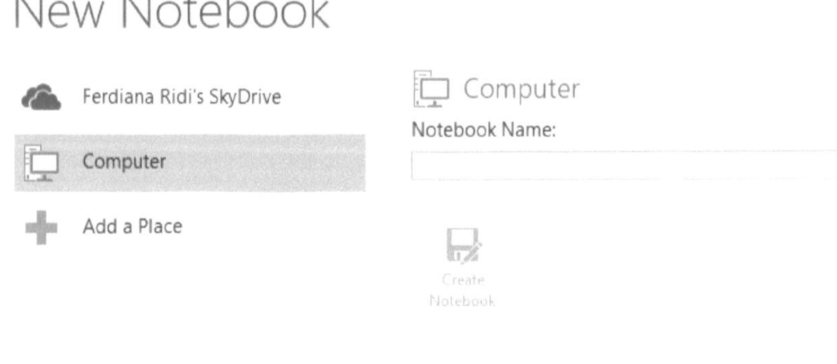

Figure 21 Creating new notebook

4. You will have a notebook called MyResearchLog. MyResearchLog notebook contains a section and a page. We can add section and page by clicking + sign as shown in Figure 22. Section is described as a category of our notebook. It can be a subject, a category, or anything. Each section has one or more pages. Each page will have a subject, a date that automatically saved, and a content.

Figure 22 OneNote User Interface

5. Content in OneNote can be text or multimedia. Basically, you can insert any content to OneNote including picture, video, audio, files link or even embedding a file. Figure 23 shows the Insert Ribbon on OneNote.

Figure 23 OneNote Insert Menu

6. If you have more than one devices, you can save your OneNote notebook to a SkyDrive. Storing notebook in SkyDrive will give you an access to any devices including smartphone and web. We will discuss SkyDrive further in Chapter 4. You can save your local notebook to SkyDrive by selecting File, Share, Choose SkyDrive, and give a name for your Notebook. Figure 24 shows the sharing feature in the OneNote. When you share a notebook through SkyDrive, you can limit the share model from yourself or your peer. We will discuss this in SkyDrive sharing feature.

7. In the other hand, you can share the several content of your research to your relative through email or blog. You can do this by selecting menu File and Send.

8. The export feature also help you to change notebook format into Microsoft Word, Adobe PDF, or Microsoft XPS for better portability. You can do this by selection menu File and Export.

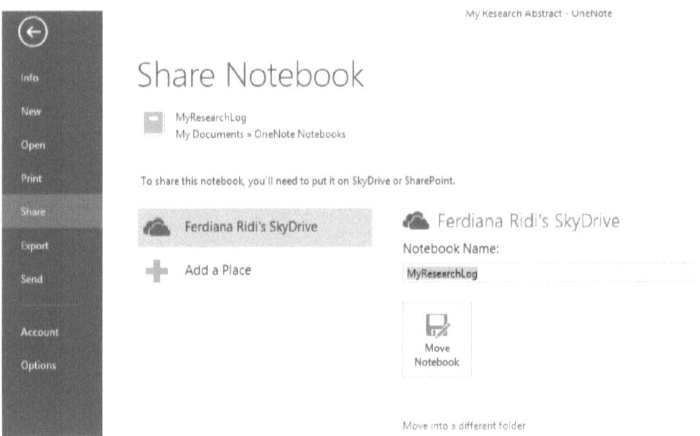

Figure 24 Share notebook in OneNote

9. OneNote supports side note taking. For example, when you are working within document and you are taking several notes. OneNote support docked windows to make you more productive. In order to do that, you can select view menu and then select docked Windows. Figure 25 shows the OneNote in docked windows.

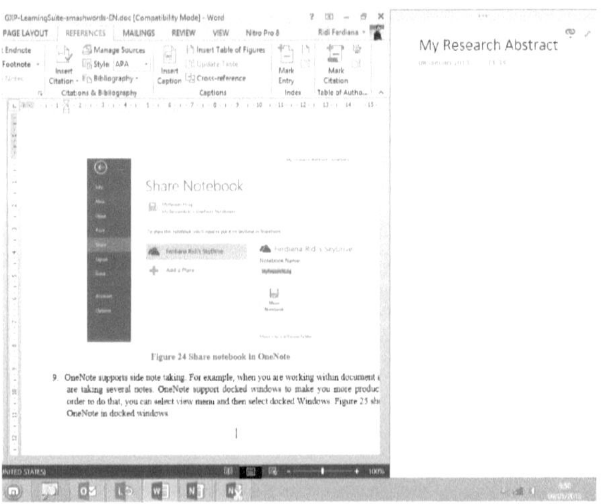

Figure 25 Docked Windows in OneNote

10. The great additional feature that you might notice is the support of translation. OneNote can read and translate it. For example we have a word in OneNote, you can select it a text that you want to

translate, select a review menu, and then select translate. Microsoft Translator will show as shown in Figure 26.

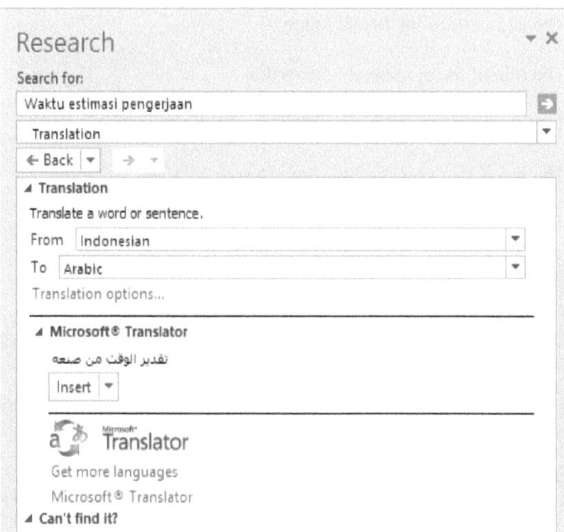

Figure 26 Microsoft Translator in OneNote

11. After creating and writing to a notebook, you might add an additional protection such as password. Password can secure a page or a section. The password itself is not recoverable, so you should save your password in safe place.

12. OneNote also provides instant drawing feature in drawing menu. If you are tablet user you can use the drawing menu to sketch and discuss anything with your peer.

OneNote is a great tool to manage your notebook, you can find similar software like Evernote and others. OneNote is your research diary, having a regular note will keep you on track on your research.

3.2 Sharing and Caring with Presentation

Teacher and student loves presentation, PowerPoint is the well-known tools for presentation. Good presentation comes from two source which are content and design. If we discuss about design, we all agree that not all people be able to create a good design. Therefore, finding a great sources of PowerPoint template should be useful. In this Section, it will discuss how to create better Presentation and communicate better with PowerPoint. You can start your own PowerPoint, you can download the free trial from http://pil-network.com

1. The first action is to find a PowerPoint template. You can search an online template in new Presentation page as shown in Figure 27. Microsoft Office Online portal has a lot of template.

What you need is the correct keywords. The tips to search better presentation is by questioning yourself about:

a. The audience of the presentation.
b. The title of the conference or session
c. The keywords of your research
d. The mood that you want to share (happy, fun, etc.)
e. The color that you want to use.

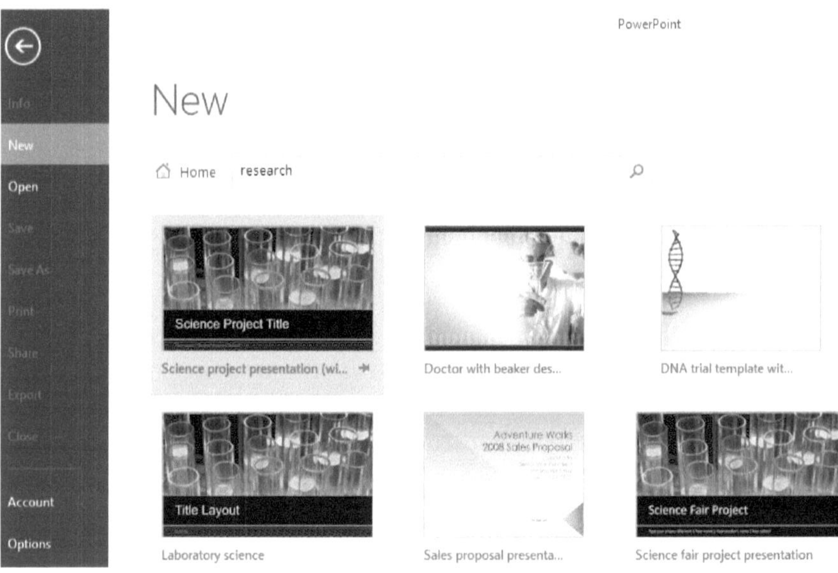

Figure 27 Online Template in PowerPoint

2. When choosing a template be sure that your template is appropriate with your presentation screen and environment. For example, if you will present in outdoor environment and the screen is limited in size. You should choose dark color rather than soft color. There are three things that you need to adjust which are color theme, color composition, and font selection. What you see on a screen might not be the same as they see in their screen. Here are the tips:

   a. Choose light color if you are on a conference room and choose dark color if you are in outdoor or a presentation with a number of audience

   b. For large numbers of audience you can use simple color composition (e.g. two main color black and white). Avoid complex color for large presentation, please use simple combination with contain only just three color or less.

   c. If you do a presentation with large audience, choose high size font with 24 point or above to make the entire audience catch your presentation.

3. Presentation should be interesting so audience will follow the presentation until the end. The key of excitement come from several sources which are

   a. Less text more message. Never copy paste from a textbook to your presentation. Keep it simple when choosing sentences. You should focus to a single message by avoiding ambiguity, using simple sentence, and one message for one slide.

   b. Picture and text. Try to combine between text and picture for a slide. This technique will draw user attention, visualize the concept, and make presentation more entertaining.

4. Practicing and creating a quick note will keep your presentation on track. Figure 28 shows you a quick note in a presentation. The note should be as simple as possible.

5. If you are only display a presentation without show a demo in your application, you can use the presenter view to display a not for each slide. In order to do that you can choose Slide Show menu and select Presenter View checkbox in monitors ribbon group.

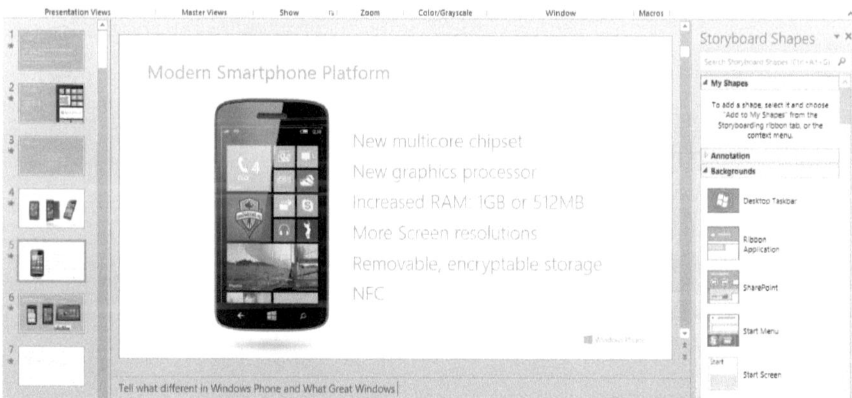

Figure 28 Picture and Text in PowerPoint

This book won't tell you the detail aspect of PowerPoint. Fortunately, you can see many book in PowerPoint. I recommend you pick one such as Microsoft Plain and Simple series that can be bought at here http://bit.ly/powerpointsimple

3.3 Creating Picture Collage for Thematic Learning

Picture is well known medium to share any idea that often better than words. A picture should have a messages that can make audience more excited with the content. In the Section 3.2, we already discuss that a picture create a good impression in the presentation.

In learning, there are two model picture representation which are single message picture or thematic picture. Single message means that the picture have a single purposes for description. Figure 29 shows the sample of single purposes picture which is studying. Single purpose picture has a strong message and really great if you put it into your presentation.

Figure 29 Single purpose picture

Thematic picture is a composition of many pictures, it provides a strong argument and abstraction of a topic. Figure 30 shows a thematic pictures about the wildlife sanctuary. In figure 30, you might see a lot pictures that combined into one picture. This one picture is called as collage. The collage is simple approach to integrate many picture into one single message. The collage can be designed using software like Paint.NET, GIMP, or Expression Studio 4. The thematic story will become a great help for audience to visualize your message.

Fortunately, Microsoft provides a tool to make a collage development easier. Microsoft AutoCollage helps nonprofessional designer to select, join, and convert many pictures into collage.

Figure 30 Thematic picture (Courtesy of PIL Network)

This article will guide you, how to create thematic picture called collage using Microsoft AutoCollage.

1. You can download Microsoft AutoCollage in http://pil-network.com , just visit Resources, Free tools and AutoCollage. In this step, you need register first to the PIL Network
2. After the installation, you shall find an icon called "Microsoft Research AutoCollage 2008". You can click the icon and open the AutoCollage.
3. The first one you should do is selecting the folder that you want to use. You should put a related picture in a folder. After you put a related picture in a folder, you can select the folder using the AutoCollage. Figure 31 shows the Microsoft AutoCollage shows videos.

Figure 31 Microsoft AutoCollage

4. As shown in Figure 31, you can select photos that will be used for Collage. You can select the entire pictures in a folder or you can select a number of photos. Microsoft AutoCollage will select a photo based on pattern algorithm. You can select "Create" button to create the Collage

5. Microsoft AutoCollage will create the Collage and will display it as shown in Figure 32. In Figure 32, it is shown the Collage result. You can save it as an image, share it, or set it as a wallpaper.

Figure 32 AutoCollage Result

Collage will be great to show a big picture concept in your presentation or demo. Collage can also be used for delivering an abstract for your demo.

3.4 Creating 3D Photo Visualization

AutoCollage provides a great way to create a thematic picture. If you need a media to display deep exploration then you can go to the video or 3D photo. If you need quick turnaround to change your still image into 3D image that would be less stressful than creating a video. 3D photo is a way to display and integrate several photos in three dimensional way. Figure 33 shows a 3D photo that shows a panoramic of a snow that you can see online at http://bit.ly/13BaRCr. Basically, a 3D photo is a way to integrate several photos into 3D like photo. A 3D photo is composed of several pictures that related and can be joined into one panoramic photo.

Figure 33 Panoramic or 3D Photos

Creating a 3D photos somewhat impossible if we don't have a specific tools. You can takes many related photo but integrate it into one photo absolutely need an extra work. Microsoft Photosynth is a tool that help you to make a panoramic photo with a guidance. This panoramic or 3D photo will help you to present a story about a situation or to show a visualization of an object or environment like a car, museum, and scenery. This Section will guide you to create panoramic photo which are:

1. Download the Photosynth at http://pil-network.com, you can see it at resources and free tools sub menu

2. You will be redirected to Photosynth site. Photosynth has two main application which are for Windows Application (desktop) and for mobile application (IOS and Windows Phone). In this tutorial, we will choose the desktop application.

3. Photosynth will be installed, you will see Photosynth icon on your desktop

4. In order to utilize the Photosynth, you should have Windows Live ID / Microsoft account. If you already registered with PIL Network, you can use that live id to join Photosynth community.

5. Photosynth community is a web site that located at http://photosynth.net/. You can see a lot of panoramic photos that made by Photosynth. In this web site, you can share your panoramic result in this web application and share your works through social media.

6. After sign in, user can create a synth. You can select photos that you want to synth it. You can add tags and descriptions. Photosynth will automatically create a synth for you. However, you should take care that the image you give is a related and continuous image, so Photosynth can provide better synth for you. Figure 34 shows you a create synth dialog.

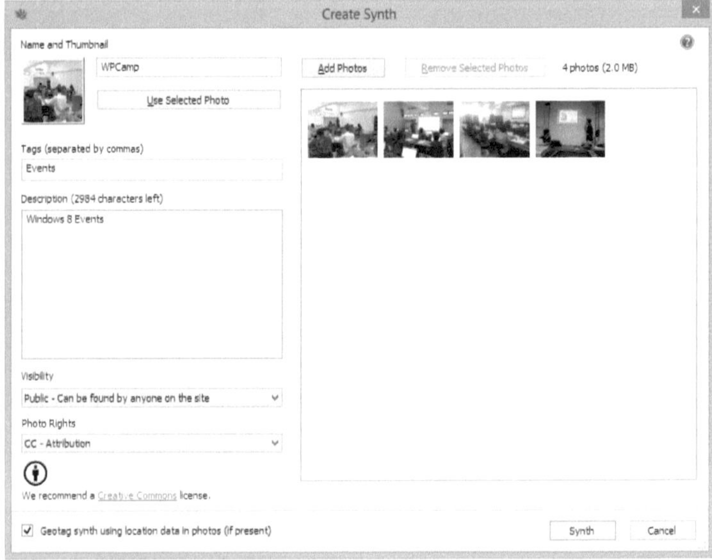

Figure 34 Create Synth on Photosynth

7. As shown in Figure 34, you can click Synth to Synth the image. There will be two condition that can be happen. The first condition happens when the uploaded images are related each other. Photosynth will create a panoramic photo. The second condition happens when the uploaded images is not really related. In this condition, Photosynth will create a good enough slideshow photo. You will know how will your images displayed by looking the synth percentage that you can see in community web site as shown in Figure 35. The higher percentage the more photo will become the first condition.

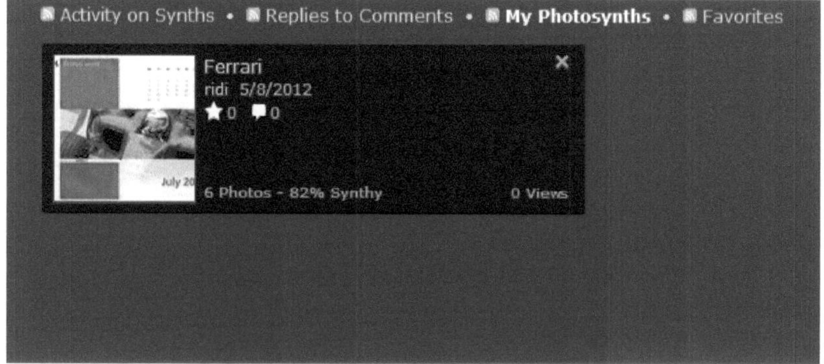

Figure 35 Synth percentage on Photosynth

8. You can see directly the result on community website or on the Photosynth application. In the end, you can share your photos to the community through social media. This approach will be good when you are delivering presentation or online material about anything that can be visualized with Photosynth.

3.5 Creating a Short Movies

Movie is great way to learn and to share. In this section, we will discuss about how to create a short movie with free tools. Movie maker and Community clip can be your friend to create a short educational movie. Before you start you should download the community clip and movie maker. Follow these steps to create a short movie.

1. Community clip can be downloaded free at http://bit.ly/communityclipsdownload and Movie maker can be downloaded at http://pil-network.com

2. Movie maker is a part of Windows Essentials 2012 (In the past, it is called Live essentials). Movie Maker in Windows essentials is integrated with Photo Gallery. Movie maker in this package is a new software that not the same with Movie maker that come preinstalled in Windows XP and Windows Vista. We recommend you to upgrade your system to Windows 8 to get better Movie maker.

3. After the installation of Community clip and Movie maker. You can capture your screen using Community clip and edit the result with Movie Maker.

4. In order to capture a screen you can select a community clips shortcut. Figure 36 shows that the community clips is running in the taskbar.

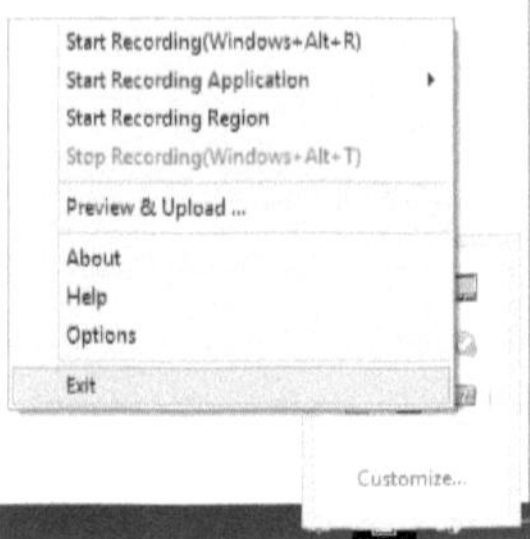

Figure 36 Community Clips

5. In order to capture a screen, you can record by selecting context menu on the icon by right clicking it.

6. Community clips has three options available which are recording the entire screen, recording the application, and recording region. If we select to record an application or a region, you should select the windows or the specific region. It will record the screen and your audio from the microphone with a dialog tells that you that the recording is in progress. Figure 37 shows the icon when active recording.

Figure 37 Recording state in Community clip

7. After recording the video will be stored as a Windows Media Video in the default storage that can be configured in Options menu. Community clip will play the video automatically.

8. The video result from the Community clip can be edited using Windows Movie Maker. In order to do that, you can add the clip from your documents by clicking Add videos and photos.

9. Movie maker will show you a story board of the clip and from there you can add another clip, add introduction, add text, or even add music. Figure 38 shows the Movie Maker

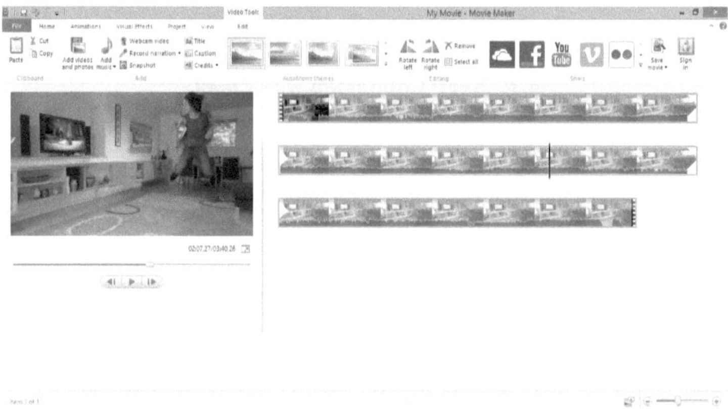

Figure 38 Movie Maker

10. There are plenty tutorial available in PIL Network about Movie maker that can be explored by visiting this site http://www.windowsmoviemakers.net/Tutorials/ . As result of your creation, you can share video to your peers using social media that well integrated in Movie Maker.

4 Managing Collaboration

4.1 Keep Connected with Email

Nowadays, email is the key of business communication. You can get it free from many provider, build it, or bought it from many providers. In this section, we will discuss how to user our email as efficient as possible using a brand new email system called Outlook email system. You can register the email new system by registering at http://outlook.com. You can follow these steps.

1. Visit outlook.com and select set it up now. Outlook is a great performance email system that support mobile, web, and client email system like an Office Outlook.

2. You can fill the required information to set up an account. After filling required information, you can see a brand new Outlook interface as shown in Figure 39.

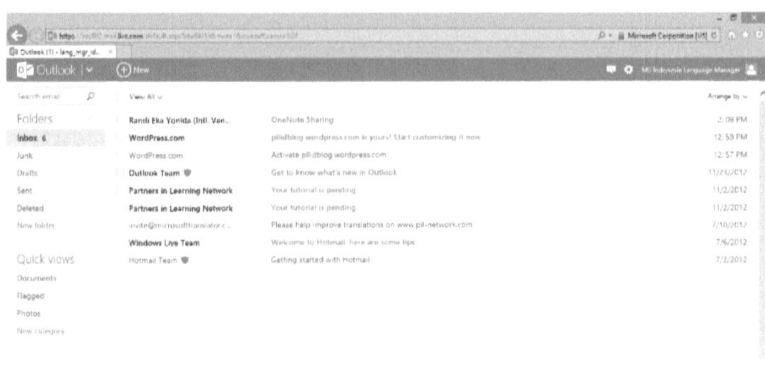

Figure 39 Outlook user interface

3. Starting from the user interface, we can create an email by clicking "new icon".

4. You have many option for this email system, you can send to your peers on Facebook or your personal contact. The personal contact can be saved through your mobile phone system, while the Facebook contact can be used through Facebook integration.

5. In order to get your Facebook contact to your account simple click the drop down menu that exist in the right of Outlook logo. You will see Mail. People, Calendar, and SkyDrive. You can click People in this menu. Outlook will show an option to integrate your account with Facebook, Gmail, an others as shown in Figure 40.

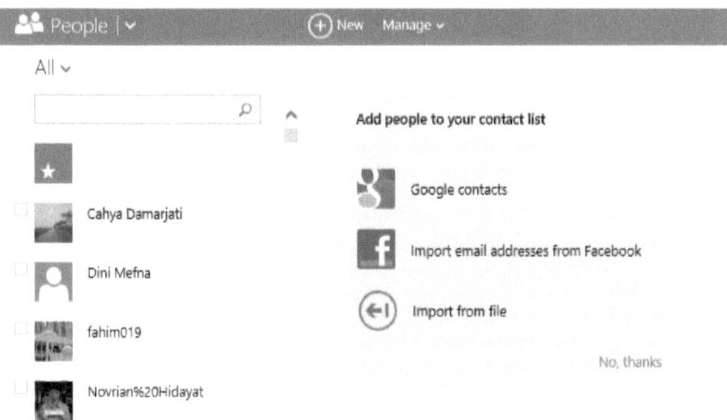

Figure 40 Contact Integration on Outlook

6. After integrating contacts, you will get benefit on contact autocomplete. You can easily add your friend email without bothering his email address. In the new email page, you can write an email and attach files to your mail. There are two methods of attachment you can upload your files to email or store your email into SkyDrive. In order to do that, you can click the clip icon, when the files are uploaded, the system will give you an option to store it into your SkyDrive. You can use SkyDrive storage if you want to reuse the files.

7. When receiving an email, Outlook has good ability to fraud check and spam stopper. For example, Figure 41 shows that fraud check on Outlook. When you get this notification, you should be careful about the validity of the email. Especially when they are requesting private information from you.

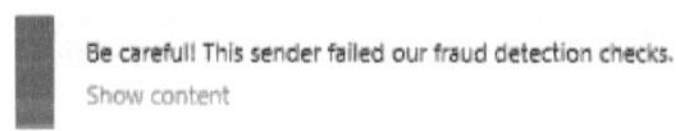

See: http://social.msdn.microsoft.com/Forums/en-US/winappswithcsharp/thread/4a776e8c-0e10-4f03-908f-7f765d914080

Figure 41 Fraud check on Outlook

8. Just like others email system, you can set rules for your mail. You can filter a specific email to be forwarded, moved into a folder, removed, or move to the junk. In order to do that you can click a setting menu (symbolized as a gear icon), select "more mail setting". You will see a lot option that can be used to customize the email behavior as shown in Figure 42.

9. As shown in Figure 42, Preventing Junk email helps the user to manage the behavior of Outlook spam assassin. Customizing Outlook will help user to manage the email folder and sorting. Reading and Writing email supports user to manage a message view. Managing your account will help users to manage the behavior of the account such as POP3 access, email forwarding, or vacation replies.

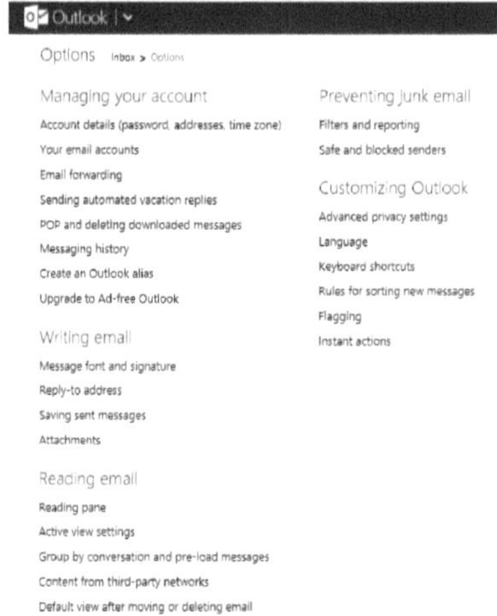

Figure 42 more mail setting on Outlook

10. Just like any other modern web email, Outlook supports messaging with peers or your contact. You can use your Outlook email to chat with your Facebook friends. If you already connected your email with Facebook, you can start chat by clicking your messaging icon as shown in Figure 43.

Figure 43 Messaging Feature on Outlook

The Outlook web mail also supports email clients and smartphone. Many smartphone like Android, Windows Phone, and Blackberry has a native configuration for Outlook email. You can visit Outlook help page at http://bit.ly/13H5ktO to configure the Outlook account.

4.2 Storing your Content to File Storage

Files are the most important things in your computer. Your document, your presentation, even your games are stored in files. Computer user should have many files in a year and some of them are important. The important files should be backed up to others device like DVD, USB Storage, or online. This section gives you tips to store your important files to an online storage system called SkyDrive. SkyDrive is an online storage that can be used for free. Microsoft gives you 7 GB for free and you can pay several dollars if you need more storage. In my point 7 GB is more than enough if just put a document on it. However, if you are multimedia author you might need more space and you can get additional space. Some of SkyDrive veteran already have 25 GB for free. If you are new to the SkyDrive you can follow these steps.

1. Visit http://skydrive.live.com , you can login with your Microsoft Account / Live ID / Outlook account. You can also visit SkyDrive thorugh your Outlook email account from Section 4.1

2. If this is your first time user, you can see an Option dialog to know what you have. You can do by clicking Option icon (Gear symbol) and than select Options menu. You will see you have several menus as shown in Figure 44.

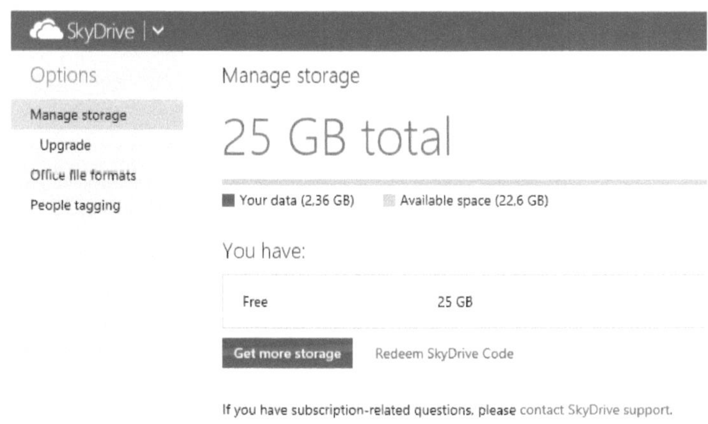

Figure 44 Options Menu

3. In Figure 44, you can upgrade your storage, set default document creation behaviour, and people tagging feature. Upgrade your storage gives you an option to increase your storage by small amount of money starting from 45 GB. Office file formats sets a SkyDrive behaviour when you create new document from the SkyDrive. Office 2007 format is default option for Office file formats. People taggings feature gives you a default behaviour when you tags or tagging by someone.

4. After seeing an option, we can see the default view of SkyDrive. You can do that by clicking SkyDrive icon. Figure 45 shows your default view of SkyDrive. SkyDrive view works like a Windows Explorer. In the left side, you can see several category of your files which are all of your files, shared files from the others user for you, your recent document, and groups document.

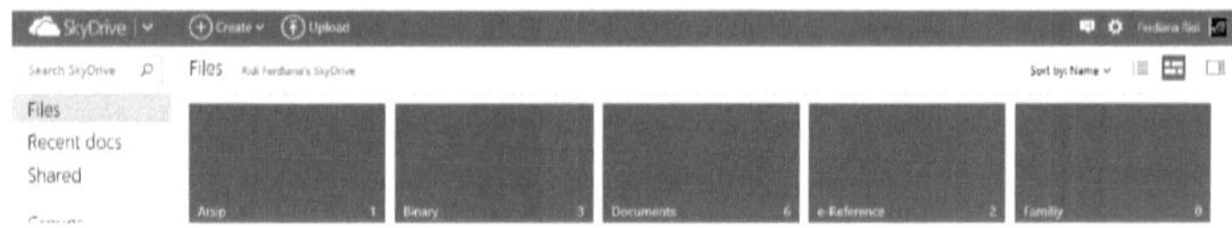

Figure 45 SkyDrive user interface

5. As shown in Figure 45, you can sorting files and changes document view. Document view can be switched to list view or icon view. In list view, you can see a detail of documents. An icon views support a slideshow if you put a picture in your files.

6. You can create a new document by clicking create icon (+ symbol). Otherwise, you can upload any files to your SkyDrive. If you click Create icon, you can create a folder, Word, Excel, PowerPoint, and OneNote.

7. SkyDrive has a good reason to support a new file from Word, OneNote, etc. SkyDrive supports you to work collaboratively with your friends. For example, you can create a new OneNote files, shares to your peers, and works together with a same file.

8. Let's we create a new Folder to learn basic SkyDrive feature. In order to do that, you can click the create icon and click Folder. New Folder will be created for you. You can give a name called "Backup"

9. Click the folder that already created for you. Let;s we drop any document to your browser. SkyDrive automaticaly upload your document. Figure 46 shows the upload process.

Figure 46 SkyDrive upload progress

10. SkyDrive supports multi file upload. You can select several files and do "drag and drop" to your browser.

11. If you need to share a file or a folder. You can do that by right clicking files and click sharing. A sharing dialog will be shown as Figure 47. In this dialog you can send email, post to social media, get a link to share. In this step, i will share a link by clicking get a link. You can get a link for view only (the visitor can't edit your files), view and edit only ((the visitor can edit your files), and public (any user including non authenticated user can access your files).

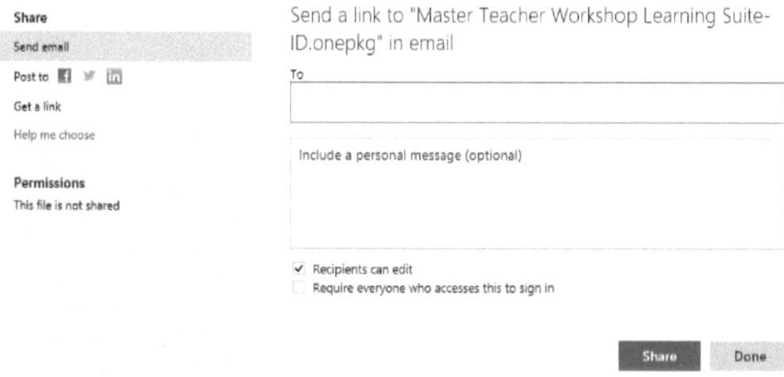

Figure 47 Sharing Dialog in SkyDrivee

12. Sharing can become a most important feature when you want to collaborate with your peers. You can select a folder to share all files in the folder. You can share a OneNote link, if you want to share a OneNote file to your peer. If you share a file with a Word, OneNote, Excel, and PowerPoint format, Microsoft Office supports to open the document without downloading first.

13. SkyDrive has Office Web Apps integrated to its system. It means you can Open Office document directly without Microsoft Office installed to your system. You can do that by selecting Open in .... menu. Figure 48 shows Office Web Apps in action. Office Web apps supports edit and view your document. The good part of Office Web Apps is a support for automatic saving. So when the connection is offline, Office Web Apps will save it automaticaly.

14. Beside sharing you can also embed your files for your online activities such as to your blog or your web application. You can do that by right clicking a folder or a file and select Embed menu. You can click Generate button to create the HTML tag. The tag can be copied to your blog post or your web. Figure 49 shows the embedded document on my personal website. Visitor can click the file and it will be redirected to your SkyDrive.

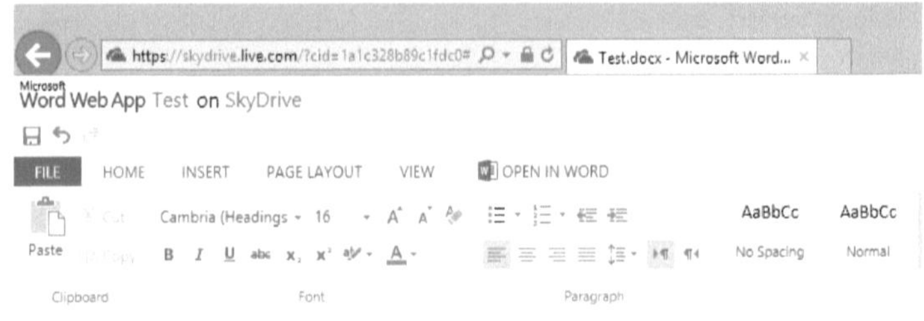

Figure 48 Office Web Apps

Figure 49 Embedding SkyDrive file

In this section, we dicuss how to use SkyDrive. In Windows 8 or Office 2013, SkyDrive has a dedicated application called SkyDrive app. SkyDrive will support you to backup your files without opening web browser. We will discuss it at Section 4.4

4.3 Get in touch with Online Presentation

The effective way to share a knowledge or to learn more topic is by presenting your idea to the audiance. Presentation is a good way to share your knowledge to your peers. In the internet era, presentation activity can be done thorugh online presentation. This section will dicuss how to create an online presentation thorugh a simple and effective way. Presenting your idea through online media like a live streaming often called as live meeting. Recorded live meeting that can be enjoyed offline often called as screencast recording. There are plenty way to create and to organize online meeting. This section will use PowerPoint and Skype to enable online presentation.

1. The first step you should have PowerPoint 2010 or later. You should also have Microsoft Account to use Skype feature. Skype is an instant messaging that can be use to call your Skype friend, landline, screen sharing and others.
2. You can download PowerPoint at http://pil-network.com and Skype at http://skype.com
3. Let's open PowerPoint and create a good presentation based on Section 3.2.
4. You can share to present online by clicking File, Share, Present Online. Figure 50 shows how to share your presentation online.

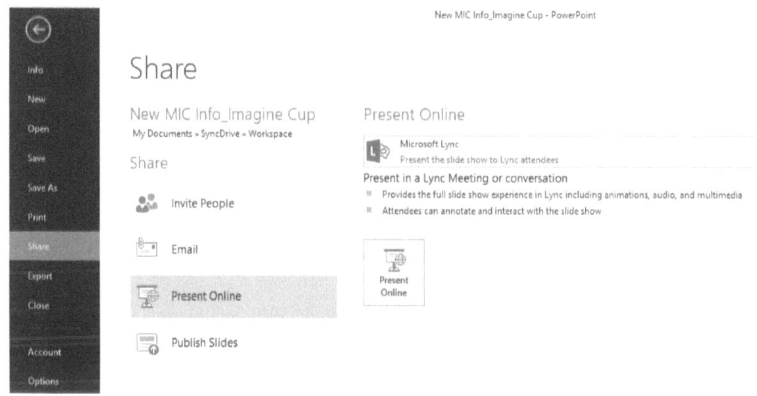

Figure 50 Share presentation online

5. Share presentation can be done with two approaches which are using Microsoft Lync or using Office broadcast. If you need audio and video conference support we can use Lync. But if you don't need the multimedia support you can use Office broadcast to do that.
6. Lync can be used by registering a service called Office 365. Office 365 can be accessed http://office365.com. There is a small investment to join Office 365, but if you are in educational organization you can get Lync for free. Unfortunately, we don't discuss Lync in this book.
7. We will do a presentation with Office broadcast. However, Office broadcast server doesn't support audio or video so your presentation seem dulls to display to your audience. As a trick, we can combine Office broadcast for presentation with Skype as an audio carrier.

8. You can login and register to Skype account by visiting https://login.skype.com/account/signup-form . The good news is you can use your Microsoft Account / Outlook web mail as an account. You just need to sign in with Microsoft account and you already join the Skype.

9. You can arrange a meeting by inviting several people that already join with Skype. You can start creating group of meeting by clicking Contacts and Add to Group. You can do drag and drop to invite them. Figure 51 shows creates group feature in Skype

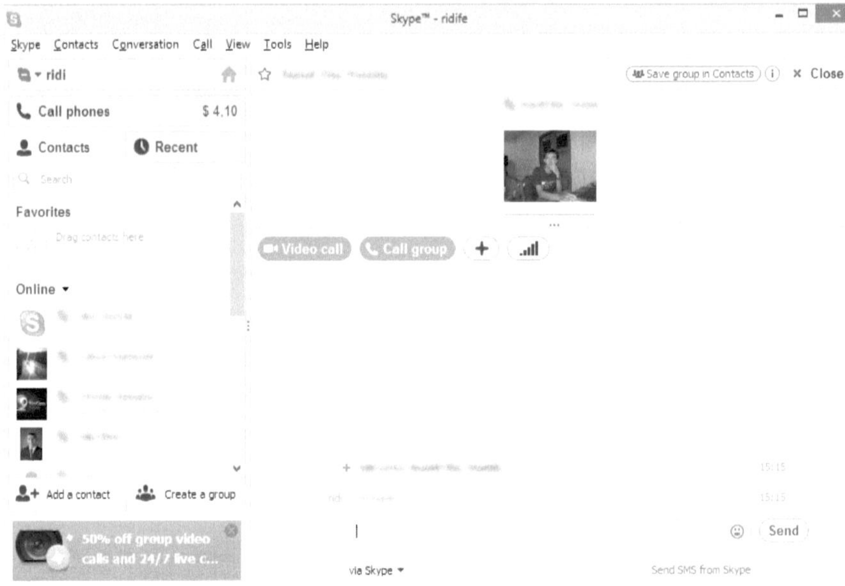

Figure 51 Skype Group Chat

10. There are no limitation to add people on a group but you might be notice that a video call is not supported for free. In this section, we use call group to deliver audio support. After you add a people on a group you can save it as a specific group name.

11. After creating a group you can start a PowerPoint, click File, Share, select Office Broadcast and Present Online. You will get a broadcast link.

12. The broadcast link can be shared to Skype IM chat. After that, the presenter can navigate the presentation while he talk the content through the Skype group call.

13. The audiences can asks question through chat box.

14. There are a situation where you need to share a whole screen to the audiences. This activity can be done through Lync application. However, if you can't afford Lync because your organization

doesn't enroll the Office 365 you can use Shared View application. Shared View application can be downloaded at http://pil-network.com

Online presentation can be good alternative when we want to create a distant learning. Distant learning can be started using this simple technique.

4.4 Synchronize Between Devices

This section discuss a solution for a simple problem which is files synchronization. For example, you have four devices which are your notebook, your pc, your tablet, and your smartphone. If you have files that you need to access from many devices you should have a copy of the files for each device. The problem arises when you update a file and you should re-copy the file to the others device. The copy and update activities will become a hassle. This section will discuss how to use SkyDrive for your daily storage synchronization. SkyDrive supports many platforms such as Windows, Windows Phone, Android, IOS, and others. This section assumes that you are using Windows 8.

1. You should register yourself for SkyDrive service. SkyDrive service already discussed in Section 4.2

2. Visit http://windows.microsoft.com/skydrive and click Download SkyDrive Apps. SkyDrive app is a brand new application that works for Vista, 7, 8 and Mac OS X.

3. After the installation you will get a SkyDrive icon in your start menu. If you click the icon. SkyDrive will open in the taskbar as shown in Figure 52. SkyDrive application work as an extension of our explorer.

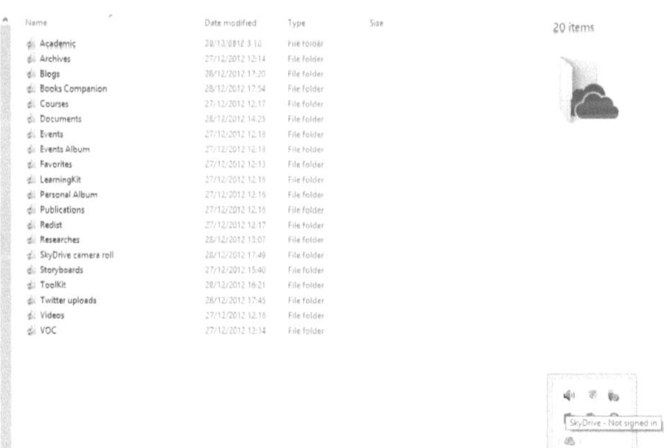

Figure 52 SkyDrive Application

4. Let's right click the SkyDrive icon and then select Setting. You will have a setting dialog for various configuration as shown in Figure 53. In Figure 53, you can sync the entire SkyDrive

folder or choose what you need. If you are new SkyDrive user, this option is good to start, but if you already put a bunch of files in there you can select which one that you should be synchronized.

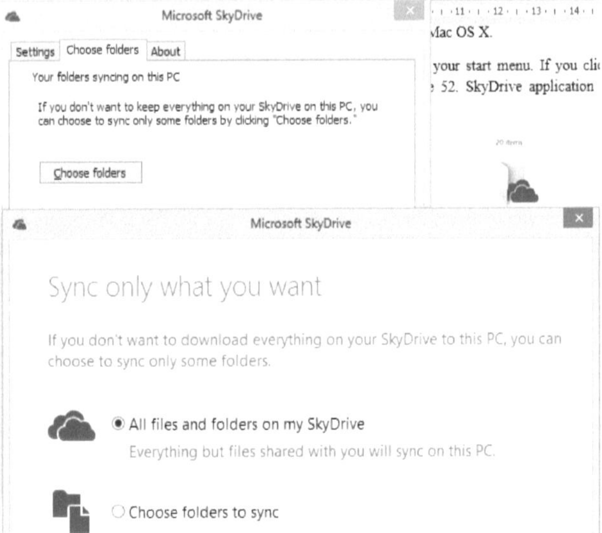

Figure 53 SkyDrive App configuration

5. The files itself can be found in favorites folder. You can access it through directly to your user documents that is located as a default location on C:\Users\(Name of User)\SkyDrive.

6. The good part is as long as the SkyDrive application is active on your computer, The files that you change locally will be reflected to the SkyDrive storage in the network.

SkyDrive application is a good way when you need a Synchronization features of SkyDrive online storage with your PC. SkyDrive also has a pro version that come with Office 2013. The pro version supports an integration with SharePoint. SharePoint is a web portal that can be used as a paperless office or document collaboration. We won't discuss SharePoint in this book, so it will be enough for us to Sync our files with this version of SkyDrive.

4.5 Collaboration Management

Collaboration is the key of successful learning. Collaboration provides a good way to share a knowledge between peers and to discuss any good learning topic. The key of collaboration is a management collaboration. For example, you want to create a virtual event with Skype and PowerPoint you. You need to send an invitation and organize who can visit your virtual events. This article will discuss about how to manage a collaboration appointment with your Outlook web account. This activity somewhat important for you to connect with your peers, arrange a face-to-face meeting, or remaindering a deadline. This section assumes that you already registered to Outlook web mail (Previously called Hotmail) at http://outlook.com .

1. Open your Outlook web mail by signing with http://outlook.com

2. After sign in, select Calendar menu by clicking dropdown menu on Outlook menu as shown in Figure 54

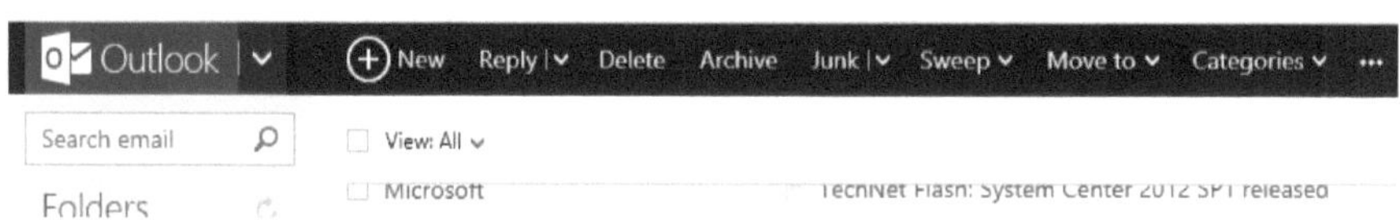

Figure 54 View a menu by clicking dropdown symbol beside Outlook logo

3. You will be navigated to Calendar system. If you are in hurry you can also directly visit http://calendar.live.com to visit Calendar system. Figure 55 shows the Calendar system.

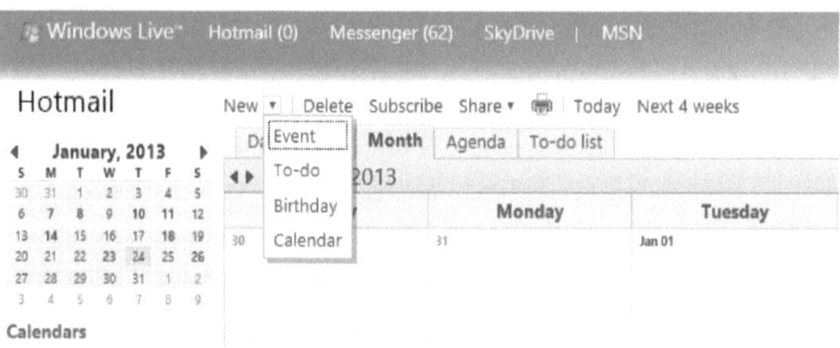

Figure 55 Calendar System on Live

4. There are four main activity that can be created in Windows Live Calendar which are event, to-do, birthday, and calendar. Event is a casual activity if you want create an event activity such as seminar, classroom, and meeting. To-do is a good way to remind a task that need to be done. Birthday helps you to remind a birthday of your colleague. The last but not least is Calendar. Calendar will support you have multiple calendar on a system. For example you can create multiple calendar for academic, professional, and personal.

5. As shown in Figure 55, let's click Event sub-menu in New. Calendar web will show you an event dialog. You can click Add more details to show dialog as shown in Figure 56. You can fill necessary information such as event description, time, and detail of the event like agenda, create recurrence, and invite the people to join your event.

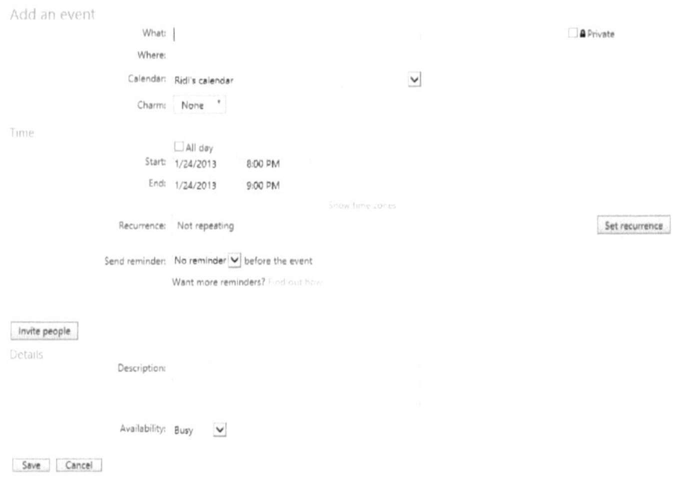

Figure 56 Event dialog on Live Calendar

6. If you click invite people, live calendar will display you a box of an email address. You can invite more than one people. When you click save button you will be notified to send an invitation to the attendee. Click Send button to send an invitation.

7. The participant of your event will receive an invitation email. The participant can set the response as accept, tentative, or declined. Figure 57 shows the invitation email on Outlook 2013.

8. If participant select accept, and he send the response now. You will see in the event detail who will be come to your event. You can see the event detail by visiting the Live Calendar, click the event name in the Calendar user interface, and you will see who's coming by clicking the "who's coming" link. Figure 58 shows the summary and who's coming link

9. Using the same dialog in Step 8, you can also update the event, cancel the event, or even add more attendees.

10. If you need prepare something for the event and you need to be remaindered. You can use "to do list" feature on Live Calendar. In order to do that, please select new, click To-do, and click add details. The dialog like Figure 59 is shown on your screen.

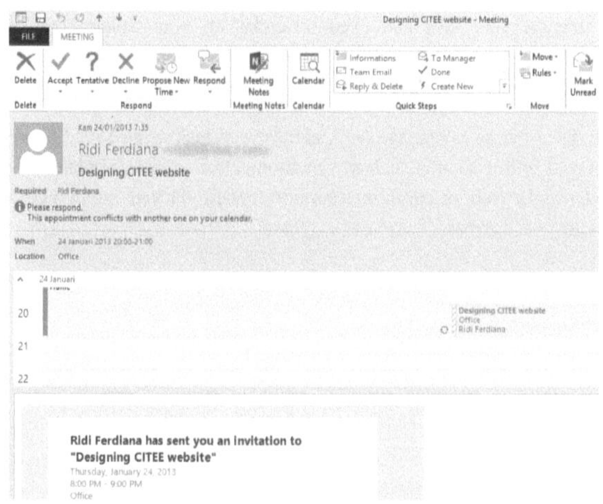

Figure 57 Invitation Letter displayed on Outlook 2013

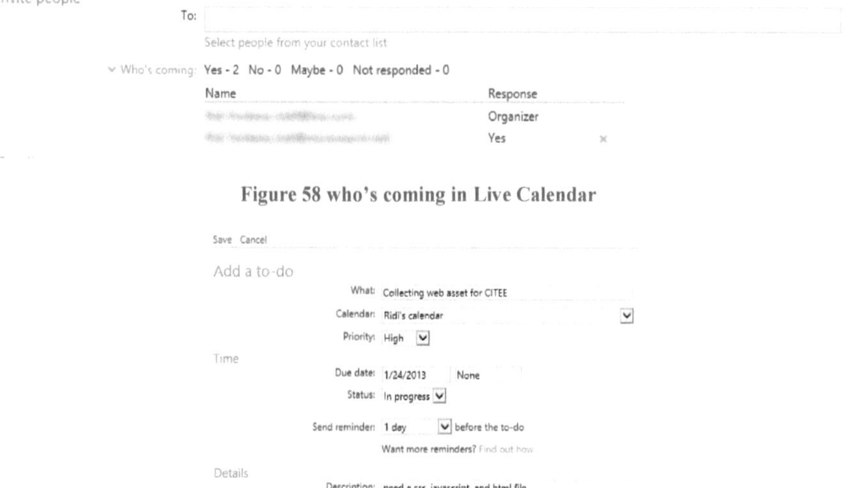

Figure 58 who's coming in Live Calendar

Figure 59 To-do dialog on Live Calendar

11. You can manage your task and event calendar on your Smartphone, Tablet or event your computer that can be utilized the Live Calendar. However this Section won't cover that activity since the heterogonous of the devices.

In this section, we discuss how to manage our Calendar and task using Live Calendar. There are a lot of option that not covered in this section such as synchronization your live calendar with your smartphone, embed your calendar to the web, or configure reminder system through email. Feel free to explore, if you feel lost just visit http://windows.microsoft.com/hotmail

5 SHARING KNOWLEDGE

Having known something is definitely good but sharing to the others it will be a great experience. Sharing is not about transferring your knowledge but it also validate and enrich your existing knowledge. Teaching is not about giving a material, is about sharing and discussing a knowledge that you get and reshape the knowledge for better insight.

This section focuses to enhance your sharing experience through a curriculum and teacher toolkit. Digital literacy curriculum provides a holistic way how to get basic knowledge of IT for learning. Teacher toolkit provides a good start for teacher who want to teach with the technology.

5.1 Digital Literacy Curriculum Sample

Digital literacy can be considered as a basic knowledge for teacher, student, and society to learn IT for their daily need. Microsoft provides free e-learning and certification for a student and teacher through http://bit.ly/digitalliteracycertification. There are three curriculum that can be learned which are basic, standard, and advance. Basic curriculum is a good way to know about computer. Standard curriculum is a curriculum that contains basic curriculum plus internet and web knowledge. While Advance curriculum is a standard curriculum with additional information to use digital information effectively. You can share digital literacy for anyone who interested with computer. Digital literacy can be learnt online through Microsoft e-learning platform or can be learnt offline through downloaded material. This section will discuss step by step to use Digital literacy e-learning opportunity.

1. Visit http://bit.ly/digitalliteracycertification with your browser.
2. You should select a language that you want to use for learning experience. There are more than 20 languages that can be chosen. Figure 60 shows the language selection. In this section, it will be chosen an English language and Advanced curriculum.
3. There are no primary requirement that you should finish the basic course before the advanced one. You can select the course without constraint.

Figure 60 Digital literacy curriculum website

4. Digital literacy provides you two model of learning which are offline learning and online learning. Offline works great when you don't have broadband internet connection. However, you should download the learning material first before you learn the activity. Figure 61 shows the learning dialog that gives you an option to download the learning kit or to view the e-learning version.

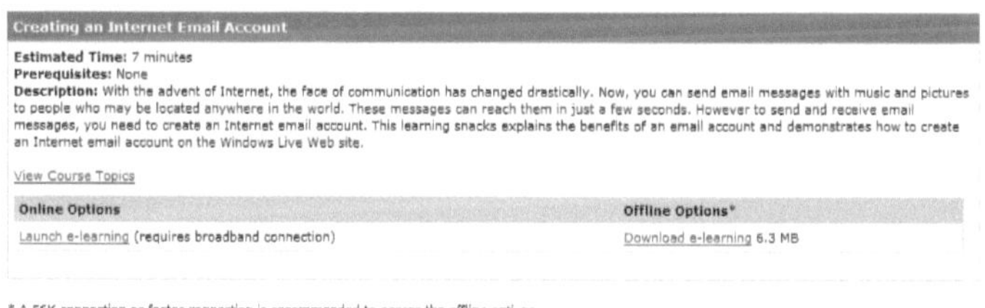

Figure 61 Digital literacy learning experience

5. In order to get Digital literacy certificate, you should finish the online assessment. It will be a good idea to download the material to learn offline and then finish the online assessment.

6. The learning platform that build for digital literacy e-learning is powered by Microsoft E-learning. If you already have done e-learning with Microsoft you should be really familiar.

Microsoft e-learning consists of learning navigation on the left, learning content type on the bottom, and learning material on the center. Figure 62 shows you Microsoft e-learning platform.

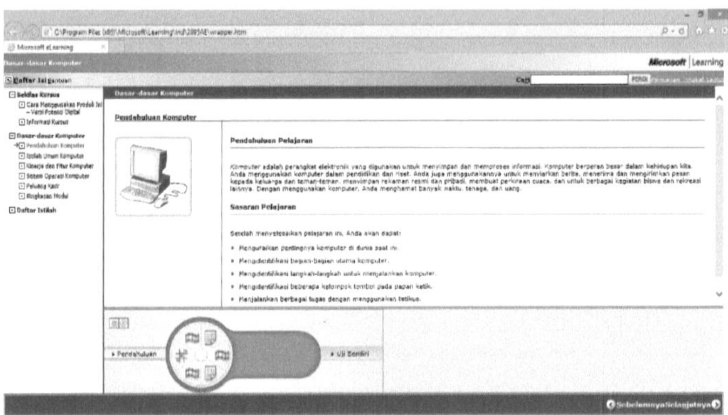

Figure 62 Microsoft E-learning platform

7. After watching and learning materials, you can join the assessment. The assessment works online, you should have at least 64 Kbps internet connection. The assessment mostly contains a multiple choices as shown in Figure 63.

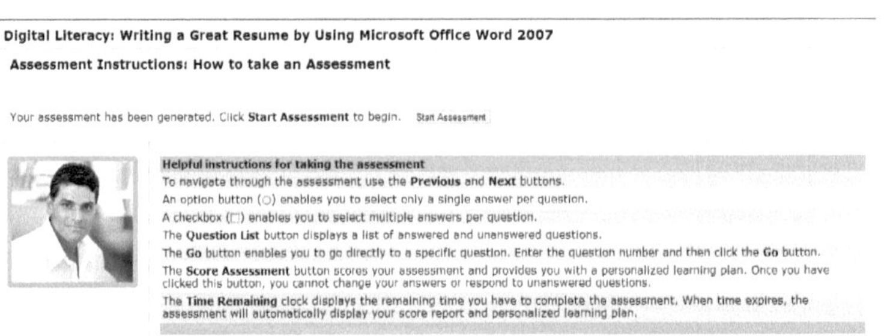

Figure 63 Digital literacy assessment

8. You should pass any assessment to receive a digital literacy from Microsoft.

In this section, it discusses a free e-learning certification called Digital literacy. It provides a citizen a structured learning material to learn basic activity of IT. It depends on the need of the learning, they can learn a basic, standard and advanced.

5.2 Innovative Teacher Toolkit

Productive Learning with Microsoft Learning Suite

Innovative teacher toolkit is a good way for a teacher or a person to learn how to be better teacher. Innovative teacher toolkit provides a set of tools for a teacher to teach with information technology. PIL-Network provides innovative teacher toolkit in several resources which are on Learning suite, critical thinking guide, and accessibility guide. Innovative teacher toolkit on learning suite provides a basic understanding to plan a class, to execute a class, and to review a class. Critical thinking provides a teacher to improve student critical thinking. Accessibility guide provides a basic understanding for a teacher who teaches to the student who have learning disabilities and different learning style.

In this section, it will explore a handful guide through resources from PIL-Network.

1. Innovative teacher toolkit can be downloaded from Learning Suite. Therefore, in order to download the innovative teacher toolkit, it should download Learning Suite first from PIL-Network.

2. Innovative teacher toolkit can be downloaded at Teach section on Learning Suite application launcher. Figure 64 shows the Learning Suite launcher.

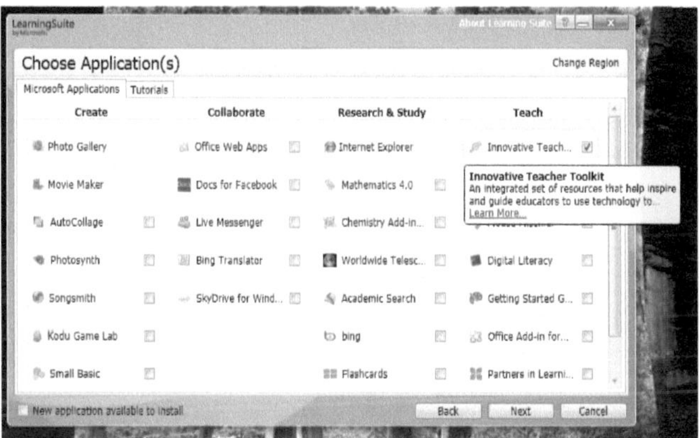

Figure 64 Learning Suite launcher

3. Learning suite will download the Innovative teacher toolkit. After the installation, user can access the innovative teacher toolkit through Learning Suite menu. The launcher will display a browser as shown in Figure 65. Innovative teacher toolkit contains three main area which are skill that should be gave for 21st century, lessons for specific skills, and tips to teach well.

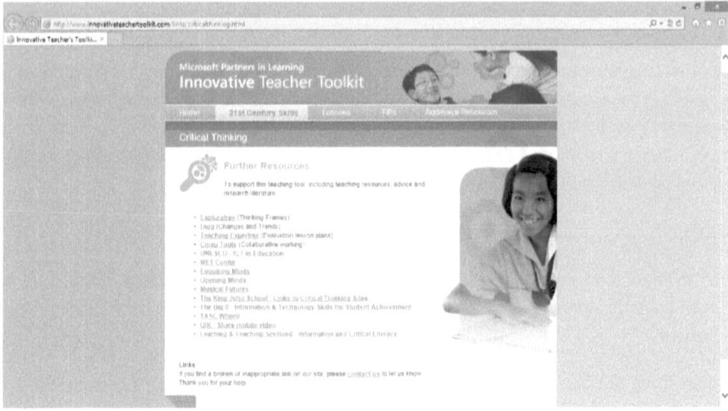

Figure 65 Innovative Teacher Toolkit

4. Innovative teacher toolkit provides one stop shopping that a teacher should be understand. One great resources is about a skill that a teacher should have in 21th century. It provides unique way to teach. For example, there is a technique called exploratree. Exploratree is a good technique to plan an exploration class. Figure 66 shows the Exploratree as a tool to create a learning plan.

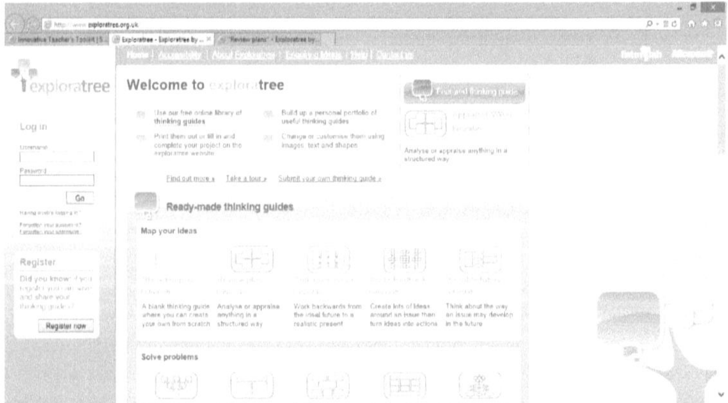

Figure 66 Exploratree as a tool to create a learning plan

5. In others menu, we can see a lot of learning resources in lesson menu as well as additional information that redirect to the internet sources. Lesson menu provides a guide way to adopt specific skill such as human right skill, multimedia and others. The tips provides quick material for specific tips in teaching. Figure 67 shows the additional menu for Innovative Teacher Toolkit.

Figure 67 Additional menu on Innovative Teacher Toolkit

6. Another good resources that related with teaching skill is to create a critical thinking for student. This resource can be downloaded in PIL-Network as PDF file. It contains 37 pages guide that give basic knowledge for a teacher to improve student critical thinking. Figure 68 shows the front page of critical thinking guide.

Figure 68 Student Critical Thinking guide

7. The last resource is about a tips to improve learning experience for student disabilities or unique learning experience. It provides a documentation about how to provide student accessibility for vision impairments, learning impairments, mobile impairments, and others impairments. Figure 69 shows the guide that can be used for teacher to improve their learning technique for disabilities student.

Microsoft

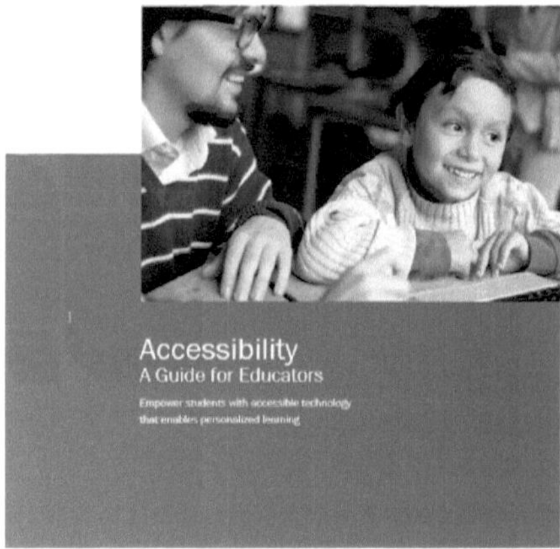

Figure 69 Accessibility guide for teacher

This section provides many resources for a teacher to become the next generation teacher. Innovative teacher toolkit provide a basic skill to teach a student, improve student critical thinking, and provide better learning experience for disabilities student. Learning those resources provides a better visibility for teacher to teach student in effective way.

5.3 Sharing a Good Picture for Better Visualization

Sharing is caring, if you share something positive that push a society to become productive. As a teacher or instructor, there is many way to share your idea. One of the good sharing media is through a picture and social media. In this section, it will discuss how to share a good picture with Windows Photo Gallery. Windows Photo Gallery can be downloaded for free in Windows Essentials. Photo Gallery is a bundled product with Movie Maker. Therefore, Photo Gallery works well on Vista, 7 and 8.

1. Photo Gallery is social based photo viewer. It means you can edit, improve, and share your photo to social media. Figure 70 shows Photo Gallery user interface.

2. As shown in Figure, you can edit the photo, view as a slide show, tagging people, add metadata, and share it into email or social media such as Facebook, Twitter, and others. The sharing feature can be accessed in Share box in Main menu.

3. If you are the first time user you should add several photos from devices such as camera, removable storage, or scanner. It can be done by clicking import button ass shown in Figure 70.

4. Photo gallery will display photos and videos that located in Picture and Video Library. You can also add the location that contains of photos and videos by right clicking tree navigation on the right.

5. As a photo editor, Photo Gallery has several built-in editing features such as rotate, resize, crop, noise reduction, straighten and many more. It can be explored in Edit menu.

Figure 70 Photo Gallery user interface

6. The special menu in Photo Gallery is located on Create menu. Create menu provides additional way to create exciting photos such as panoramic photo (integrating several continuous photos into one image), AutoCollage, Photo Fuse, and others features that can be downloaded later. Figure 71 provides a Create menu on Photo Gallery

Figure 71 Create menu on Photo Gallery

Photo Gallery is a good way to edit photos and share it into your peers. Imagine that you can share your mind map idea, inspired image, or good education video with your peers. It will have a good effect for their learning idea.

5.4 Sharing a Thought by Writing a Blog

Writing a good way to share. If you love to share your idea to anyone on the internet. Blog is a good media to share your idea. Blog is a web application that provides a mechanism to post anything that you want. You can post short article, post a new tutorial, or event post a video. In this section, we will discuss how to create a blog and use Windows Live Writer to write a blog. By writing a blog, you can learn to write and get better visibility with others.

1. Live Writer can be downloaded as a part of Windows Essentials software package that can be downloaded free at http://windows.microsoft.com/en-US/windows-live/essentials-home. The latest version of Windows Essentials is Windows Essentials 2012.

2. There is a writer application that will help you keep productive to share your idea. Writer is a blog editor that support many blog interface such a WordPress, Blogger, BlogEngine, and many more. Figure 72 shows Writer application

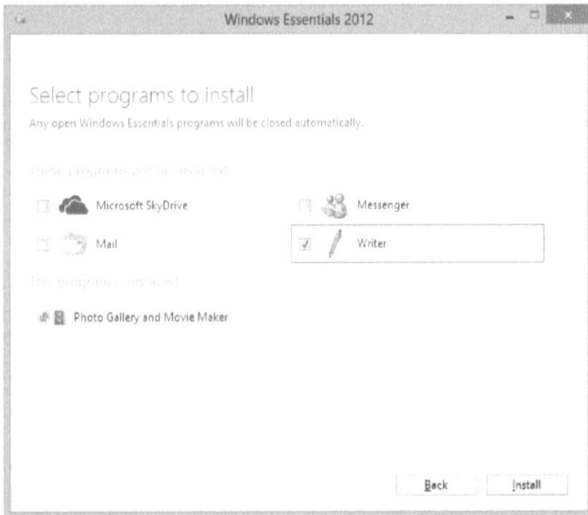

Figure 72 Writer Application

3. After installation, Writer will request a blog information that already you have. If this is your first time to have a blog, you can visit http://wordpress.com to create a new blog.

4. The wizard will show you an option to select blog provider, user authentication, and any additional information. Figure 73 shows the dialog box of writer wizard

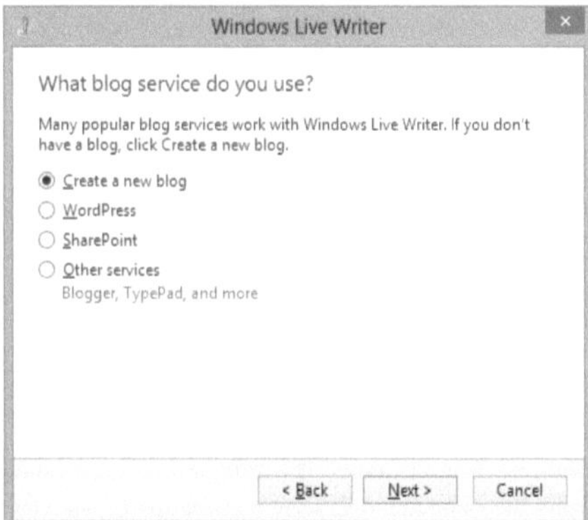

Figure 73 Blog service selector on Writer

5. After the configuration, Writer will download the necessary files for the blog writer user experience. The configuration will be finished after you give a short name for the blog.

6. Writer is just like a word editor, so you will use same editor model. The Writer result is a html document that can be edited manually or use graphical notation as shown in Figure 74

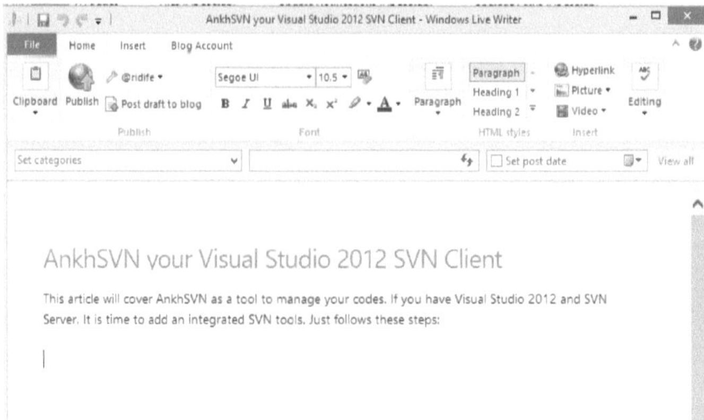

Figure 74 Blog editor on Writer

7. After writing a blog post, user can save to server as draft or publish it directly. User can also insert any additional content such as video, image, and others. The multimedia content will be

uploaded along with the blog post automatically. The behavior can be changed through manage blog account that can be accessed through Publish Ribbon as shown in Figure 75.

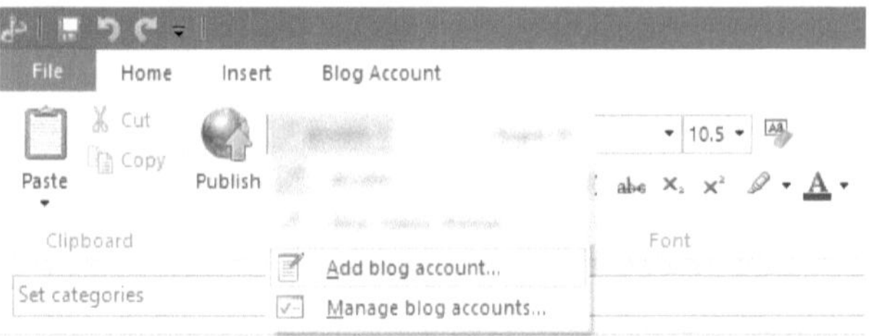

Figure 75 Manage blog accounts

8. Writer supports multiple blog accounts. It means we can use more than one blog account in a writer instance. Using the same menu as shown in Figure 75, user can switch from one blog to the other and add new blog into this account.

9. The last good thing about writer is plugin capability. Writer has a bunch of plugin that can help you create appealing blog post. Plugin can be visited in Insert menu and Add plugin. Writer will redirect to the plugin page http://bit.ly/X55iW0. In this page user can download and install free plugin such as insert a file plugin, access SkyDrive plugin, and many more

This section provides a basic guide to create a blog and update it with quality post using Live Writer. Blog can be great way to share your idea through the internet and Writer help you to share the idea with more productive way.

6 Epilogue

This pocket book purposes is to introduce you several technology that enable you to learn and share more effectively with information technology. Hopefully, this book not only become reference for teacher but also provide additional information for any learner that closely related with the internet.

Learning is something that work continuous. Internet can be source of anything that you can learn further. In this section, it will discuss two main website that should be used as a learner references. The websites are Partner in Learning website and Microsoft IT Academy website.

6.1 Partner in Learning

Partners in Learning network or PIL-Network is initiative that developed by Microsoft and academic partners to create learning community ecosystem. PIL-Network provides teacher, student, and community to create a social media based on learning interest. The PIL-Network can be accessed through http://pil-networks.com. PIL-Network supports multiple language based on Bings translation, so any teacher who is not capable to use international language like English, can use their local language. Figure 76 shows the PIL-Network website.

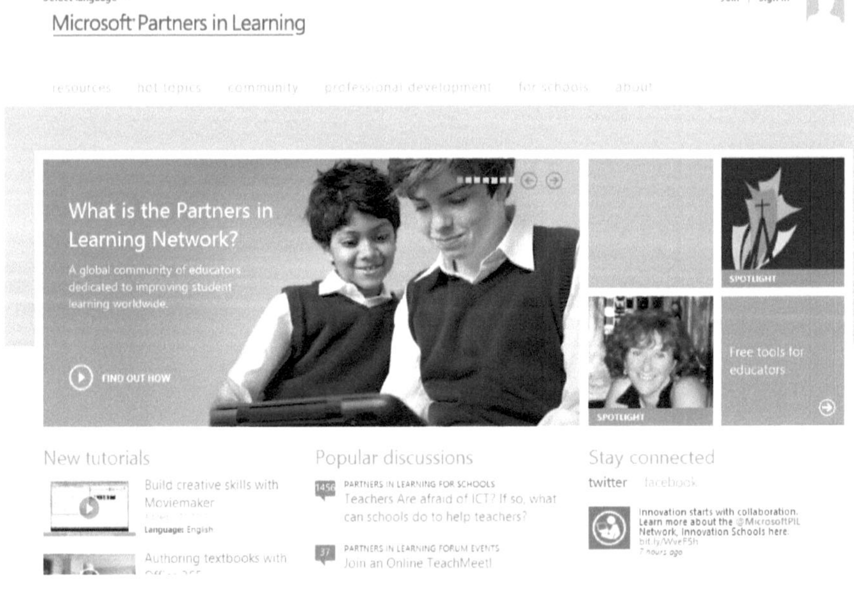

Figure 76 PIL-Network website

PIL-Network has several basic menu such as resources, hot-topic, community, professional development, for schools menu, and about PIL-Network. The description for each menu is described as follows:

1. Resources composed with several useful resources such as free tools, Tutorial, and learning activities. Free tools is the most demanding menu in PIL-Network. It provides free software like a Learning Suite and others. There is a learning activity as well as tutorial from teacher to teacher. Learning activities exposes what can be done with technology in a classroom. While tutorial is a short video about learning something. Both tutorial and learning activity can be uploaded by members.
2. Hot topics provide a latest technique to teach and to share. In this page, teacher can see many case studies from teachers around the word about learning technique and others.
3. Community provides a specific forum for teacher and faculty who want to share anything about learning material, learning technique, case studies and others.
4. Professional development is just like a learning reward and achievement for the teacher. Teacher can learn two professional development courses. Earn points and get a badge to show about his competence.
5. For school menu provides an opportunity for a school to join PIL-Network program in school. This just directory where student and teacher in this organization adopt several technology and techniques from PIL-Network.
6. About menu provides additional information about PIL-Network program.

The good point of the PIL-Network is providing you the latest tools and course to always stay ahead as a teacher. Tools and Professional development can be used for free to improve teacher skill. The professional development adopts several standards such as UNESCO ICT and others. There are curriculum, e-learning, and assessment that can be done in PIL-Network. Figure 77 shows the Professional Development in PIL-Network.

Figure 77 Professional development on PIL-Network

6.2 Microsoft IT Academy

Productive Learning with Microsoft Learning Suite

Competition in education today is quite high. The educational institution need to provide a strong qualification for tomorrow education. It means that educational institution should aware about what society need in term education and how educational institution provides the best qualification of their student.

IT academy provides additional value in education for the student and education organization. The Microsoft IT Academy provides students with the future ready technology skills they need to be successful in college and a career. IT academy can be seen at here http://www.microsoft.com/itacademy/. IT academy is dedicated for student and teacher who teach IT as a basic or additional curriculum. IT academy provides curriculum, certification, educator tools, and lab software.

IT academy has several basic curriculum for several IT competency such as Office productivity, Web design, software development and others. IT academy provides three basic which are e-learning, lesson plans, and academic courseware. Figure 78 shows the ready to use material on IT academy

1. E-learning provides a flexible learning delivery through Microsoft E-learning. E-learning provides a getting started guide for Microsoft certification.
2. Lesson plan is a good way to introduce basic concept in technology on a short tutorial. Lesson plan provides short and quick tutorial about basic need of technology such as Windows, Microsoft Office, SharePoint and others.
3. Academic courseware is a good way to implement IT in a coursework such as intensive course or courses. It takes about 6 to 16 weeks learning, It compatibles with IT curriculum such as game development and others.

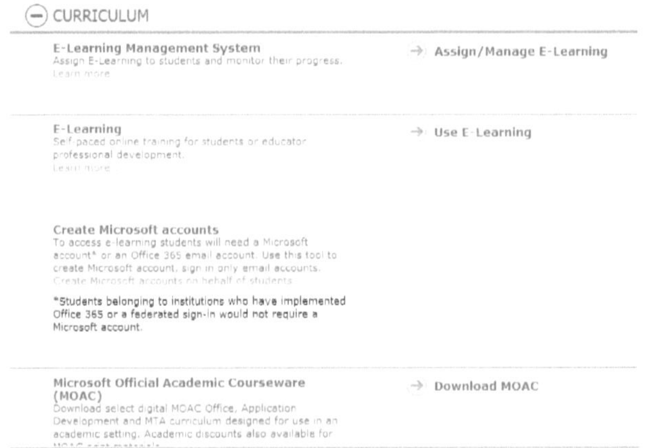

Figure 78 Curriculum on IT Academy

IT academy solves basic problem for education organization to improve IT additional skills for student. For example, if a student can graduate with a good GPA, he can get better value if he also has certification. Microsoft provides many certification for student like Microsoft Technology Associate

(MTA) and Microsoft Certified Professional (MCP). By having a certification, student or teacher will have a more visible competency than others that don't have certification.

1. MTA is dedicated as undergraduate student certification. It provides basic certification such as Windows, Web, Software Development, HTML 5 and others. You can learn more about MTA at http://certiport.com/mta
2. MCP is professional certification for student or graduated student. It covers real world certification such as MCTS (Microsoft Certified Technology Solution), MCPD (Microsoft Certification Professional Developer), MCITP (Microsoft Certified IT Professional), MCSD (Microsoft Certified Solution Developer) and many more. This certification somewhat important for student future career if they focuses in Microsoft Technology adoption. http://microsoft.com/certification is one stop web site to see the huge selection of new Microsoft certification. Figure 79 shows the Microsoft certification page

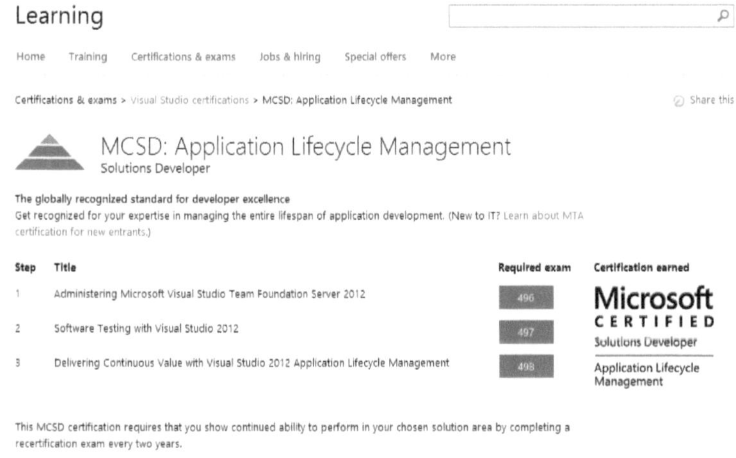

Figure 79 Microsoft certification on Microsoft Learning page

The last but not least IT Academy provides a software for learning such as Microsoft Windows, Office and others. The software can be activated through a program called DreamSpark. DreamSpark is eligible for IT academy subscriber or Microsoft campus agreement subscriber. Figure 80 shows the DreamSpark that covers a lot of Microsoft software from OS, Server, and others.

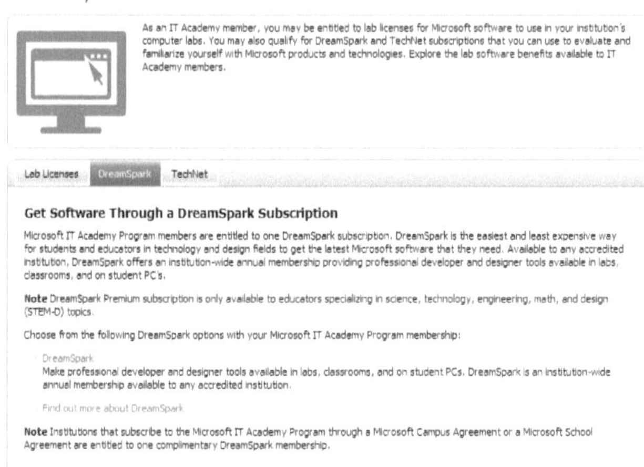

Figure 80 DreamSpark on IT Academy

This section discuss how academic organization improve the IT adoption through structured course and program. IT academy provides an organization to eliminate the hassle to build a material, create a lesson plan, and evaluate the student competency.

6.3 Useful Links

Below is a quick links for any related content in this book.

1. Home page PIL-Network: http://www.pil-network.com/
2. Join/sign-in PIL-Network link: http://www.pil-network.com/signin
3. Free tools: http://www.pil-network.com/resources/tools
4. PIL-Network tutorials: http://www.pil-network.com/resources/tutorials
5. Learning Activities: http://www.pil-network.com/resources/learningactivities
6. PIL Community: http://www.pil-network.com/discussions
7. Photo Gallery download: http://windows.microsoft.com/en-US/windows-live/
8. Movie Maker download: http://windows.microsoft.com/en-US/windows-live/
9. Microsoft OneNote download: http://www.microsoft.com/en-us/download/details.aspx?id=30354
10. World Wide Telescope: http://www.worldwidetelescope.org/ExperienceIt/ExperienceIt.aspx
11. Photosynth: http://photosynth.net/
12. Skype for Education: http://education.skype.com/
13. Microsoft SkyDrive: http://windows.microsoft.com/en-US/skydrive/download
14. Outlook Mail: http://outlook.com/
15. Microsoft IT Academy: http://www.microsoft.com/itacademy/

www.ingramcontent.com/pod-product-compliance
Ingram Content Group UK Ltd.
Pitfield, Milton Keynes, MK11 3LW, UK
UKHW041918190726
13854UKWH00003B/1316

9 781300 641292